I0800833

IMAGES
of America

Kane County
The War Years

The Kane County Illinois Veterans Memorial was dedicated on the grounds of the Kane County Government Center in Geneva, Illinois, on November 11, 2004. The memorial's Wall of Honor is a list of the names of Kane County's sons and daughters who have died while on active duty from the Spanish-American War to the current conflicts in the Middle East. (Author's collection.)

On the Cover: Taken in 1920, this image shows returning World War I veterans from St. Charles and Kane County in front of St. Patrick's Church in St. Charles. (Courtesy of St. Charles History Center).

IMAGES
of America

KANE COUNTY
THE WAR YEARS

Kevin J. Gaffney

ARCADIA
PUBLISHING

ISBN 978-1-4671-2570-3

Published by Arcadia Publishing
Charleston, South Carolina

Printed in the United States of America

Library of Congress Control Number: 2016955963

For all general information, please contact Arcadia Publishing:
Telephone 843-853-2070
Fax 843-853-0044
E-mail sales@arcadiapublishing.com
For customer service and orders:
Toll-Free 1-888-313-2665

Visit us on the Internet at www.arcadiapublishing.com

To the Kane County veterans of World War I and World War II who served valiantly and in many instances paid the ultimate sacrifice with their lives in training and on the battlefield.

Contents

Acknowledgments

A special thank-you for the many hours of image and research assistance provided to the author goes to Mary J. Manning, McCormick Research Center, Cantigny First Division Museum, Wheaton, Illinois; Yolanda Weisensel, Camp Grant Museum, Rockford, Illinois; Alison Costanzo, St. Charles History Museum; Jennifer Putzier and Michael Fitchtel, Aurora History Museum; and Elizabeth Marston, Elgin History Museum. Thank you, to Arcadia Publishing for considering this topic for publication and to Liz Gurley for her encouragement, review, and title management.

Finally, a heartfelt thank-you goes to my grandfathers Joseph C. Gaffney and Frank J. Corrigan, who both served as models to me through their lives, love, courage, grace, and humility, despite their enduring World War I, the Great Depression, and World War II. Another man who has greatly influenced me throughout his life is my uncle James L. Corrigan, who served valiantly during World War II, flying several dangerous missions in Europe in a B-24 Liberator as part of the 506 Bomb Squadron, 44th Bomb Group. Another uncle, James A. Gaffney, served as a captain in the 91st Reconnaissance Division, fighting in battles against the Germans in North Africa and Italy, ultimately being awarded the Purple Heart. Finally, I will always cherish the love and encouragement my mom and dad, Mary Ellen and Charles, showed me—always inspiring me in my academic pursuits, love of history, writing, music, public service, and my faith.

This picture depicts my grandfather Joseph C. Gaffney in his World War I uniform. Following World War I, he served the community of St. Charles as park board president for nearly 25 years, as St. Charles Chamber of Commerce president, and on the board of the St. Charles Savings and Loan. He was also offered a contract to play baseball with the Chicago Cubs in 1912, but could not do so due to assisting his mother, Jane Moore Gaffney, who was widowed. Later, he was instrumental in starting up boys' baseball in St. Charles and, as a result, has a softball field named in his honor at Pottawatomie Park in St. Charles. He and Karl Gartner were both honored in 1973 with the highest city award, the Charlemagne Award for community service, by the St. Charles Chamber of Commerce. (Author's collection.)

INTRODUCTION

Kane County, Illinois, was established in 1836 and named after Elias Kane, a US senator. The population of Kane County in 1900 was 78,792, increasing to 99,499 at the end of World War I. Preceding World War II in 1940, Kane's population had grown to 130,206. In 1900, approximately 99.20 percent of the population of Kane County were Caucasian. Additionally, in 1900, about a third of the people living in Kane County resided in rural areas. Therefore, it is not surprising that farming was a critical part of the economy. Between 1860 and 1950, the percentage of large farms with an area of at least 500 acres grew by approximately 180 times. Post–World War I, the total number of farms in Kane County was 2,248. In 1917, Kane County was similar to many of areas of the United States in that it was rural and agricultural and its ethnicity was primarily white European.

After Woodrow Wilson's election in 1912, he sought to proclaim US neutrality upon the beginning of World War I in 1914. Even following the German sinking of the ship *Lusitania* in May 1915, killing 1,201 people, Wilson was still reelected in 1916 on a platform of neutrality and keeping America out of Europe's war. However, during the first months of 1917, Germany's aggressive submarine warfare with the sinking of the American cargo ship *Housatonic* on February 3, 1917, led Wilson to cut off diplomatic relations with Germany. Later, in 1917, Germany attempted to strike an alliance with Mexico through the German ambassador to Mexico, Arthur Zimmerman. Germany promised Mexico financial and territorial rewards for Mexico's support of Germany if the United States later declared war on Germany. The final act of aggression by Germany occurred on April 1, 1917, when the armed US steamer *Aztec* was torpedoed near Brest and 28 of its crew members died.

On April 2, 2017, Wilson asked Congress for a declaration of war against Germany and the Central Powers. Wilson stated, "We shall fight for the things which we have always carried nearest to our hearts, for democracy, for the right of those who submit to authority to have a voice in their own governments, for the rights and liberties of small nations, for a universal dominion of right by such a concert of free peoples as shall bring peace and safety to all nations and make the world itself at last free." On April 4, the Senate voted in favor of war by 82 votes to 6; two days later, the House of Representatives delivered its own yes vote by 373 votes to 50, formally announcing the entrance of the United States into World War I.

On May 18, 1917, Congress adopted the Selective Service Act for men ages 21 to 31, and in August 1918, Congress expanded the age range to 18 to 45. Before World War I had ended, 24 million men had registered; 2 million men were drafted. Pres. Woodrow Wilson appointed John J. Pershing commander in chief of the American Expeditionary Forces (AEF). By Armistice Day, November 11, 1918, there were 2.1 million American men in France.

Many of the soldiers of Kane County served in the 33rd Infantry Division, including but not limited to the 129th and 130th infantry regiments under the 65th Brigade. The 129th was commanded by Col. Charles H. Green, and the 130th was commanded by Col. John V. Klinnin. The 66th Infantry Brigade contained both the 131st Infantry Regiment commanded by Col. Joseph B. Sanborn and the 132nd Infantry Regiment commanded by Col. Abel Davis. The 33rd Division was formed under the command of a native Illinoisan, Army general George Bell Jr. The 33rd Infantry Division was also known as the "Prairie Division." The 129th Infantry Regiment was drafted into service on August 5, 1917, and assigned to the 33rd Division on October 12, 1917. The earlier regiments, 11th and 12th now making up the 129th, had served valiantly during the Civil War. They were again reorganized and mustered into service during the Mexican border dispute on June 29, 1916, at San Antonio.

The 131st Infantry Regiment, initially known as the First Illinois Infantry, originated in Chicago on August 25, 1874, and was made up mostly of Civil War veterans. The regiment volunteered to fight in the Spanish-American War, and on June 30, 1898, it fought and held the line between Teddy Roosevelt's "Rough Riders" and the First District of Columbia Volunteers. The regiment also served in the Mexican border dispute in 1916, and then on October 1, 1917, it was renamed the 131st, US Army, a unit of the 66th Brigade, 33rd Division. The Illinois National Guard and regiments of the 33rd Division were mustered to camps in northern Illinois, including Camp Deneen in Elgin and Camp Grant in Rockford. Eventually, most of the men in the 33rd were transferred to Camp Logan in Houston, Texas, before being shipped overseas for action.

On May 9, 1918, the 131st left Camp Logan in Houston and passed through Camp Upton, Yaphank, Long Island, and then boarded the ship *Leviathan* on May 20. On May 30, the *Leviathan* was attacked by four German submarines, but escaped. Two of the German subs were destroyed, and one surrendered. The converted passenger ship transported over 119,000 soldiers as of November 1918 between the United States and Brest, France. The 131st spent its first night in the port of Brest, France, on May 30.

The activities and battles of the 33rd Division in Europe began on July 4, 1918, Companies A, C, E, and G of the 131st Infantry took part on the attack on Hamel. This was the first time American troops had ever fought alongside the Australians and with the British in any action of significance. The Americans charged to the shouts of "Lusitania!" On August 8, 1918, the 131st, led by Colonel Sanborn, broke the German line at Chipilly Ridge and Gressaire Wood, the Somme Offensive. On August 23, the 33rd Division was transferred by rail from the British front to the area of the First American Army in the Toul Sector and later in the region of Tronville-en-Barrois. On September 5, the 33rd Division started for Verdun and eventually relieved the 120th French Division. The 33rd Division was the first American division to hold a portion of the front line on that historic battlefield. September 26, 1918, marked the beginning of the Meuse-Argonne Offensive wherein the 33rd formed the right of the 111th American Corps being led by Maj. Gen. Robert Bullard. The major German positions being held between the Meuse and the Argonne were the Montfaucon and the Bois de Forges. These positions were thought to be impregnable by the Germans. However, after only three hours and thirty-three minutes, the 66th Brigade—composed of the 131st, 132nd, and the 124th Machine Gun Battalion being led by Col. Joseph B. Sanborn, Col. Abel Davis, and Maj. Floyd Putman, respectively—captured the German positions and their many machine gun nests. On October 6, 1918, the 33rd Division was transferred to the French 17th Army Corps and the 1st and 2nd Battalions of the 131st, including Companies A and D, 124th Infantry under the command of Col. Abel Davis participated, along with the French, in the attack east of Meuse. The 66th Brigade held the left sector west of the Meuse River from October 15 to October 21, then was relieved by the 15th French Colonial Division. Forty-four days elapsed from the time the first unit of the of the 33rd Division entered the trenches at Verdun until the last troops had left. Upon being relieved, the 33rd then marched to the Saint-Mihiel front. Raids by the 131st against Saint-Hilaire on November 8 as well as the 130th led to the German stronghold of Marcheville. Companies A and B of the 131st, along with the 124th Machine Gun Battalion, captured the Bois d'Harville. On November 11, 1918, the 65th Infantry Brigade, headed by the 129th Infantry, had attacked and was in possession of the Chateau d'Aulnois, Riaville, and Marcheville when the order to cease hostilities put an end to its advance. The total distance covered by the 33rd from July 4, 1918, starting at Hamel, through November 11, 1918, was 47,300 meters, or 29.39 miles. Total prisoners taken were 3,924. Full casualties of the 33rd Division were 798 KIA (killed in action), 7,299 WIA (wounded in action), 148 missing, and 18 captured, with a total of 8,263. Kane County World War I loses totaled 151 men. Aurora alone lost 85 men during this time in service. As of February 14, 2010, Medals of Honor had been awarded to 47 men, of whom 16 are dead. Of the 31 remaining, 8 belong to the 33rd Division. One hundred ten men of the 33rd Division received the Distinguished Service Cross. Additional, detailed information, including details on operations, all who served, and casualties of the 33rd Division, 131st can be found through the Illinois State Library Digital Archives.

During World War II, on March 5, 1941, all four regiments of the 33rd Division, being comprised of the 129th, 130th, 131st, and 136th Infantry Regiments, were federalized. The regiments served and fought the Japanese forces in the Northern Solomon Islands, New Guinea (January 24, 1943, to December 31, 1944), Lingayen Gulf, and Luzon and engaged in the final push and capture of Baguio (December 15, 1944, to July 4, 1945), in the Philippines. Manuel Roxas, later to become president of the Philippines, was freed during the capture of Baguio by elements of the 33rd and 37th Divisions. Casualties, including KIA, WIA, captured, and missing, totaled 2,426. A summary of the history of the 33rd Division in World War II is available from the US Army Center of Military History.

The 1st Infantry Division "Big Red One" in World War I was initially assembled on June 9, 1917, at New York City as the 1st Expeditionary Division of the AEF (American Expeditionary Forces). It was later redesignated as the 1st Infantry Division with its motto as "No mission too difficult, no sacrifice too great—duty first!" The 1st was renowned in World War I for being the first to leave the United States, the first to land in France, the first to march in Paris, and the first to fire a shot. The World War I infantry units of the 1st included the 16th, 18th, 26th, and 28th regiments, as well as the 2nd and 3rd Machine Gun Battalions. The noted division commanders and those for the 1st Infantry and 2nd Infantry Brigades, along with the 1st Field Artillery Brigade of the 1st Division, can be found in chapter 3. On June 14, 1917, contingents of the 1st Division sailed from New York and Hoboken and arrived on June 26 at Saint-Nazaire. The order of battle for the division is covered in chapter 4, but a brief summary of its major engagements follows.

By April 1918, the Germans had pushed to within 40 miles of Paris. Responding to the German offensive, "the Big Red One" moved into the Picardy Sector to assist the exhausted French First Army. On April 5, 1918, the 1st Division moved to an area of the French Fifth Army near Gisors, northwest of Paris, where it resumed training. From April 27 to June 8, 1918, the 1st occupied Cantigny Sector (Picardy). On May 28, the 28th Infantry captured Cantigny. June 9–13, the Cantigny Sector occupation merged into the Montdidier-Noyon defensive, withstanding enemy attacks, including artillery bombardment. From July 18 to July 23, the 1st participated in the Aisne-Marne Operation. On July 18, the 1st attacked east and captured Missy-aux-Bois. Later, on July 19, the 1st attacked and occupied Plouisy. From August 7 to August 24, the 1st occupied Saizeras Sector, Lorraine. It was here that the 1st was ordered to join the First Army. From September 8 to September 11, the 1st fought and held the Lucey Sector known as the Ansauville Sector, Lorraine. Later, from September 12 to September 16, the 1st, with the 26th Division, completed its advance and defeat of the enemy at Saint-Mihiel. On September 27, the 1st entered into the line east of the Argonne Forest. The 1st advanced seven kilometers and defeated, in whole or part, eight German divisions. This victory was led in part by the efforts of George C. Marshall, a captain in the 1st Division. From October 1 to October 13, 1918, the 1st attacked and advanced through the Bois de Montrebeau. From October 29 through November 11, 1918, the 1st fought the enemy to the heights of Meuse and later marched upon Sedan. From November 17 through December 12, the 1st advanced into Germany through Luxembourg, Canach, Konz, Schweich, Wittlick, Alf, and Treis, eventually arriving on December 12 in Coblenz. On July 19, the 1st relieved the 2nd Division and occupied the entire Bridgehead. The 1st was at Sedan, the farthest American penetration of the war, and was the first to cross the Rhine River into occupied Germany. By the end of the war, the division had suffered 4,964 killed in action, 17,201 wounded in action, and 1,056 missing or died of wounds. Five 1st Division soldiers received the Medal of Honor.

Following the attack by the Japanese on Pearl Harbor on December 7, 1941, the 1st Division was ordered to Camp Blanding, Florida. The 1st departed New York on August 1, 1941, and arrived in Beaminster, England. On October 22, 1942, the 1st was sent for combat and an amphibious assault of North Africa. As part of Operation Torch, the 1st as part of the II Corps went ashore in Oran, Algeria, on November 8, 1942. The 1st was led by Maj. Gen. Terry Allen and Brig. Gen. Theodore Roosevelt Jr. in combat at Maktar, Tebourba, Medjezel Bab, Battle of Kasserine Pass, Gafsa, El Guettar, Beja, and Mateur. The North Africa battles ended with the 1st helping secure Tunisia on May 9, 1943.

The 1st took part in Operation Husky, invading Sicily still under the command of Maj. Gen. Allen. Gen. George S. Patton requested the 1st Division as part of his forces of the First Army invading Italy, with the 1st ultimately being again assigned to the II Corps. The 1st took part in the Battle of Gela and then moved through the center of Sicily into some of the heaviest fighting at the Battle of Troina.

When the campaign in Sicily was completed, the 1st was returned to England in November 1943 to prepare for D-day and the invasion of Normandy. On June 6, 1944, the 1st Division, along with the 29th Infantry Division, constituted the first wave to attack the Germans on Omaha Beach. In advancing nearly 300 yards to the bluffs, casualties reached 30 percent in the first hour of the assault. By the end of the day, the 1st was able to secure Caumont and Formigny. The 1st assisted with the breakthrough at Saint-Lo with an attack on Marigny on July 27, 1944. The 1st later reached the German border at Aachen in September 1944 and then attacked through the Hurtgen Forest. From December 17, 1944, through January 28, 1945, the 1st was moved to the Ardennes front and countered the German Wacht Am Rhein offensive, also commonly known as the Battle of the Bulge. The 1st continued to battle forward through the Siegfried Line and across the Rur, driving on to the Rhine and crossing the Remagen bridgehead on March 15–16, 1945. The 1st later captured Paderborn and was in Czechoslovakia when war ended in Europe. Overall, the 1st lost 3,616 KIA, 15,208 WIA, and 664 to wounds. Sixteen members of the 1st Division were awarded the Medal of Honor.

One

War Declared in April 1917

Prior to April 1917 and America's entrance into World War I, the training of men from Kane County was ongoing since the Spanish-American War and the Mexican border conflict. Many of the men who served in the Illinois National Guard, the 33rd Division, and the 1st Division during these prior conflicts were ready for the "war to end all wars." Army and National Guard camps were prevalent throughout the United States before World War I and grew immediately after the passage of the Selective Service Act of 1917. Places like Camp Deneen in Elgin, Illinois; Camp Grant in Rockford, Illinois; and Camp Logan in Houston, Texas, to name a few, played vital roles in preparing citizens to become fighting soldiers. As Col. Robert R. McCormick of the 1st Division noted in 1918 when in France, "Fighting is the primeval purpose of the male." The task in 1917 was preparing the United States and its men for the brutality of war in Europe.

Construction of Camp Grant began on July 1, 1917, and the First Illinois Engineers, Company A arrived initially, followed by the First Illinois Infantry. On September 30, 1917, both units left for Camp Logan, Houston, Texas, for training. The 33rd Division was formed under the command of Gen. George Bell. Camp Grant remained an Army post unit January 1924, when it became the home of the Illinois National Guard. In 1940, it again became a regular Army post for use during World War II.

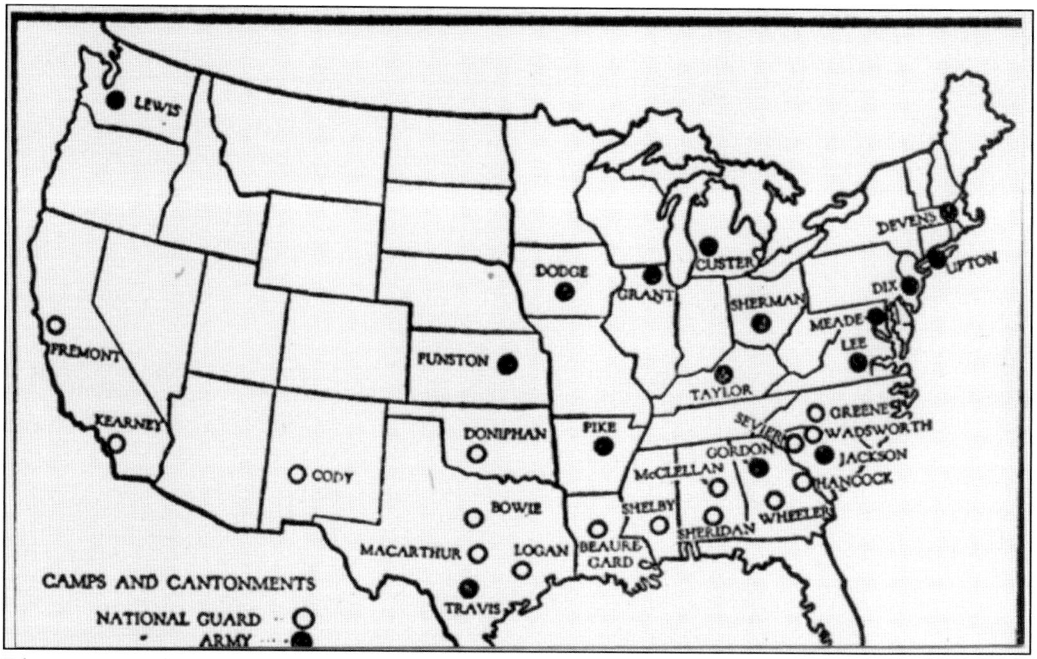

This 1917 map locates National Guard and US Army training camps including Camp Grant and Camp Logan. The soldiers from Kane County trained at various camps including Camp Grant, Camp Deneen, Camp Logan, and an officer's camp at Fort Sheridan. (Courtesy of the Illinois Digital Archive.)

The Illinois National Guard trained at Camp Deneen in Elgin, Illinois, in 1909, following the Spanish-American War and prior to the US-Mexican border dispute arising in January 1916. (Courtesy of the Elgin History Museum.)

Men of the 106th Cavalry Regiment, Illinois National Guard trained on artillery, including the 75-millimeter cannon. Camp Deneen was located at what is now Wing Park in Elgin, Illinois. (Courtesy of the Elgin History Museum.)

Troops of the Illinois National Guard parade down State Street, Elgin, Illinois, toward their encampment at Camp Deneen. Many of these men earlier saw action in the Mexican border dispute. (Courtesy of the Elgin History Museum.)

This is an aerial map of Camp Grant in Rockford, Illinois, showing barracks and other landmarks of the 33rd Division of the Illinois National Guard. The image also shows many of the training areas and barracks for the 129th, 130th, 131st, and 132nd Infantries that, after training, took part in many of the major engagements in France in 1917 and 1918. (Courtesy of the Camp Grant Museum.)

Men of all ages enjoyed some winter sports at Camp Grant during the winter of 1918 before relocation for training at Camp Logan and their subsequent deployment to France. (Courtesy of the Camp Grant Museum.)

New recruits trained at the rifle range and fired at a distance of 300 yards during the winter of 1918 at Camp Grant. Many of the men at Camp Grant were from the Midwest and had previous rifle training. (Courtesy of the Camp Grant Museum.)

Officer training at Camp Grant included learning topography and map drawing. Many of the officers of the Illinois National Guard trained also at Camp Sheridan and later at Camp Logan in Houston, Texas. (Courtesy of the Camp Grant Museum.)

2632. FIELD KITCHEN AT RIFLE RANGE, CAMP GRANT, ILL.

Men at the field kitchen near the firing range at Camp Grant served trainees after a long day of hard work. The soldiers who later worked the field kitchens in France and Germany did not have the space and time, even behind lines, to prepare warm meals for the troops. (Courtesy of the Camp Grant Museum.)

2635. RECREATION ROOM IN SOLDIERS' BARRACKS, CAMP GRANT, ILL.

Noncommissioned soldiers relax in their new quarters, reading the latest news, playing cards, and enjoying a competitive game of pool. Some of the soldiers take some time to write a letter home before their eventual transfer to Camp Logan. (Courtesy of the Camp Grant Museum.)

After a long day of training, the soldiers enjoy some competitive volleyball, relieving the stress of training and any worries about fighting in the war in France. Camp Grant was built with many opportunities for the men to engage in competitive sports. (Courtesy of the Camp Grant Museum.)

Christmastime at Camp Grant in December 1918 found officers and soldiers together enjoying the recreational room and YMCA. Many of the men read the latest news and reminisce about their loved ones at home. (Courtesy of the Camp Grant Museum.)

2637. READING ROOM OF OFFICERS' CLUB, CAMP GRANT, ILL.

The newly constructed Officers' Club included the reading room at Camp Grant. The Officers' Club displayed the various flags representing the Allied forces in World War I. (Courtesy of the Camp Grant Museum.)

Two

Kane County Sends Its Men and Women Off to War

Nearly immediately following the declaration of war by Woodrow Wilson in April 1917, the small Midwestern towns of Kane County sent men off to Europe to battle the Central Powers in France and eventually in Germany. In Kane County, 150 men paid the ultimate price in giving their lives for their country in service and battle in World War I. Approximately 56 percent, or 85 men, from Aurora, Illinois, died in service. Some died in training or in camp, of influenza, or some other illness, but most died in actual battle or later as a result of their wounds. Both world wars took their tolls on Kane County and many of its small communities. For example, in World War II, Kane County lost a total of 566, with Aurora losing 293. Known figures from St. Charles shows 28 men killed in action with an additional 35 being wounded. Many families in Kane County had multiple sons serving in both World War I and World War II (as will be noted in subsequent chapters on notable veterans from Kane County). In World War I, Aurora families that lost multiple family members in battle include the following: Cecil and Charles Curtin, Henning and Herbert Peterson, and Frank and George Wadley. World War II was no different in that many sons of the same families of Kane County served, and in some cases, died as well. Additionally, on December 7, 1941, at least seven sailors from Kane County lost their lives when the Japanese attacked Pearl Harbor.

This picture was taken in front of St. Charles High School in 1941. Students, faculty, and administrators often had multiple family members in the service. In both World War I and World War II, many families in Kane County had multiple family members in the armed services. (Courtesy of the St. Charles History Museum.)

Men from the cities of Geneva, St. Charles, Batavia, and other areas of Kane County pose for a picture before boarding the Chicago & North Western train for various training camps during World War II. Many, if not all the men, were anxious to serve after the attack on Pearl Harbor. The citizens of Kane County responded immediately to the threats posed by Japan, Germany, and the Axis forces, as did most of the country in 1941. (Courtesy of the St. Charles History Museum.)

During the summer of 1917, the excitement of the citizens of Elgin was evident as they sent off their own on a train for various training camps, including travel to Camp Grant and eventually Camp Logan, near Houston, Texas. (Courtesy of the Elgin Historical Society.)

After completing their training, World War I troops were honored with a St. Charles parade down Main Street before embarking to Europe for war. The soldiers pictured are of the Illinois National Guard. (Courtesy of the St. Charles History Museum.)

Kane County World War I Seabees, or Navy personnel, march in a St. Charles parade after training at the Great Lakes Training Center near Chicago. (Courtesy of the St. Charles History Museum.)

This building was the National Guard Armory in Elgin, Illinois. Many of the soldiers of the 33rd Division and many of the infantries of the 33rd and Illinois National Guard were initially mustered and eventually sent to various camps for training from this location. (Courtesy of the Elgin Historical Society.)

Ladies supporting the war effort played music on an Aurora parade float with a symbol of the world on the center of the float. The float is heading down Broadway in Aurora, Illinois, for the send-off of troops to initial training camps and, eventually, the battles in France. (Courtesy of the collections of the Aurora Historical Society.)

This picture captures the support of the citizens of Aurora as a send-off parade is held downtown on New York Street. Some of the participants included veterans of the Spanish-American War and prominent leaders of Aurora. (Courtesy of the collections of the Aurora Historical Society.)

Soldiers enjoyed a farewell dinner held on August 7, 1917, at Fox River Park in Aurora, Illinois. The dinner was provided to all the soldiers by the citizens of Aurora. Many of the 85 men who served in World War I, the old 129th Infantry from Aurora, are pictured here. (Courtesy of the collection of James E. Harley, donated to the Aurora Historical Society.)

Above, soon-to-be-soldiers are at the intersection of New York Street, heading down Broadway for the train depot. The parade of men is led by prominent Aurora citizens, including Webb Gould; Capt. J.H. Freeman, a Civil War veteran; and Judge Mangan. Below, a massive crowd gathers to demonstrate citizens' pride for those headed off to serve. (Both, courtesy of the Aurora Historical Society.)

Three

The Major Battles of World War I

The World War I infantry units of the 1st included the 16th, 18th, 26th, and 28th Regiments, as well as the 2nd and 3rd Machine Gun Battalions. The 33rd Division included 65th and 66th Infantry Brigades and served with five Armies and 12 Army corps including the First, Second, and Third Armies. The 1st Division was led by Maj. Gen. Charles P. Summerall, Brig. Gen. Frank Parker, Col. Omar Bradley, and Col. Robert L. Bullard, to name a few. Maj. Gen. George Bell Jr. led the Illinois 33rd Division, with the 131st Infantry being led by Col. Joseph B. Sanborn and the 132nd being led by Col. Abel Davis. Following the 1st Division's taking of Cantigny, it, along with the French and British, quickly secured ground in France for the Allies. The 33rd did likewise in major engagements also previously referenced. At Belleau Wood, the US Marines held the Germans during six days of fighting. This was followed by a major American force of 500,000 beginning its offensive at Saint-Mihiel with three days of fighting. The Americans then turned their forces toward Sedan, a highly fortified position, and fought there for 47 days. The final action with both the 1st and Illinois 33rd Divisions took place during the Meuse-Argonne Offensive, involving 1.2 million combatants wherein the Americans suffered 120,000 casualties. During this offensive, the Germans were pushed back 30 miles, with 28,000 of their troops being captured. Many of the Allied advances were attributable to the 1st Division and Illinois 33rd Division.

Gen. Benacount B. Buck and fellow officers commanded the 28th Infantry with the 1st Division in Gondrecourt, France, on August 20, 1917. (Courtesy of the McCormick Research Center, First Division Museum.)

A detachment of the 28th Infantry relieved the French in trench warfare in Gondrecourt, France, in October 1917. Many times, the 1st Division, upon arrival in France, relieved the British and French at the battlefronts, as their forces had been engaged in battle since the start of World War I. (Courtesy of the McCormick Research Center, First Division Museum.)

"Standing Toe" in the trench are troops of the 28th Infantry awaiting orders to attack in Gondrecourt, France, on October 15, 2017. These men were "seasoned," having been through many battles alongside their allies—primarily, the British and the French. (Courtesy of the McCormick Research Center, First Division Museum.)

Many of the officers of the 28th Infantry, 1st Battalion in Boursieres, France, gathered together for one last photograph before the Battle of Cantigny on April 24, 1918. This photograph was one of the first taken of the officers upon their arrival in France. (Courtesy of the McCormick Research Center, First Division Museum.)

Pictured are officers of the 28th Infantry, notably Col. Hansen E. Ely (fourth from left), who was later to command forces in battle near Abbeville, France, on April 24, 1918. At this time, the 28th and other infantries were training alongside and initially under the command of French or English generals. (Courtesy of the McCormick Research Center, First Division Museum.)

The danger is evident in this photograph as sharpshooters of the 28th Infantry engage in house-to-house combat, advancing carefully on the enemy in Bonvillers, France, on May 22, 1918. (Courtesy of the McCormick Research Center, First Division Museum.)

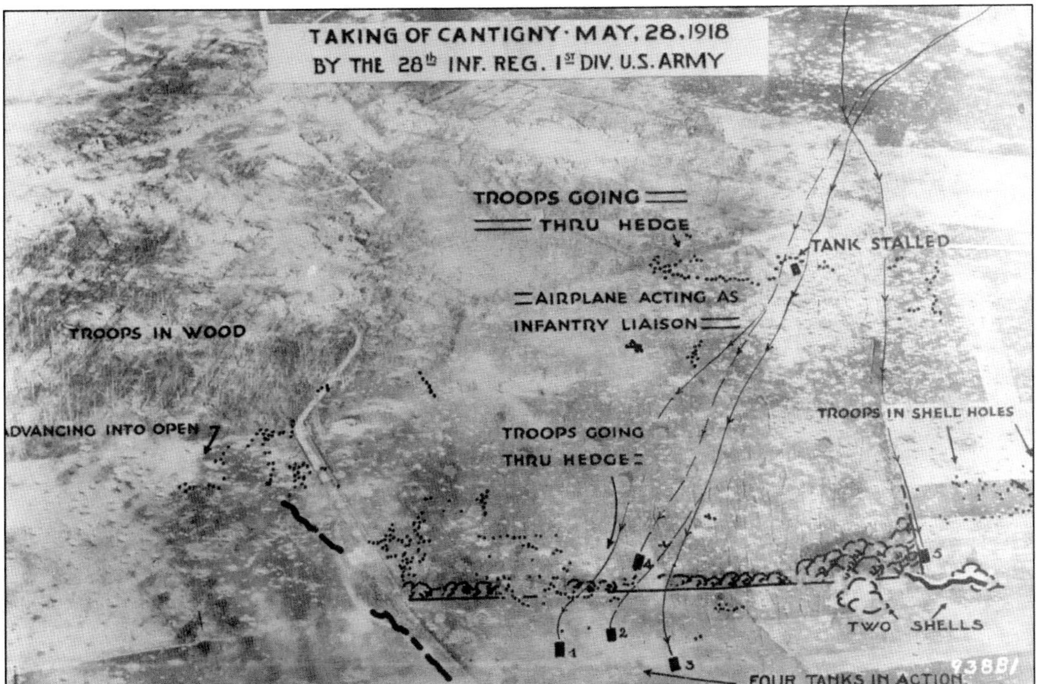

A detailed map shows the taking of Cantigny on May 28, 1918, by the 28th Infantry, 1st Division US Army. The 28th Infantry Regiment (with Col. Hansen E. Ely commanding) plus three machine-gun companies and a company of engineers (3,564 men) captured Cantigny from the German Eighteenth Army. The village was situated on high ground surrounded by woods, making it an ideal target for German artillery. (Courtesy of the McCormick Research Center, First Division Museum.)

Waves of American troops advanced on Cantigny with the assistance of French tanks on May 28, 1918. The village was taken in about 30 minutes. (Courtesy of the McCormick Research Center, First Division Museum.)

The first major American encounter with the Germans at Cantigny resulted in a decisive victory, as is evident with the mopping up of any German opposition on May 28 by the 1st Division. (Courtesy of the McCormick Research Center, First Division Museum.)

The 1st Division covered earlier battlegrounds (1914, 1915, and 1916) of the Somme Valley as the 1st advanced on its attack of Cantigny on May 28, 1918. This picture clearly shows the advance of troops into the ruins of Cantigny after being shelled by the enemy. (Courtesy of the McCormick Research Center, First Division Museum.)

Col. W.S. Grant observes artillery at Cantigny and the surrounding area prior to the 28th Infantry advancing on May 28, 1918. (Courtesy of the McCormick Research Center, First Division Museum.)

This photograph shows the 28th Infantry in the Somme Valley as the attack began on Cantigny with the assistance of the French and their tanks on May 28, 1918. The picture depicts the openness of battle and the obvious vulnerability of troops in their advance. (Courtesy of the McCormick Research Center, First Division Museum.)

A different angle of the 28th Infantry moving through the Somme attacking Cantigny features artillery bursts above the American troops as they advance. (Courtesy of the McCormick Research Center, First Division Museum.)

The results of battle and shelling are evident in this image of the remains of the village of Cantigny on May 28, 1918. (Courtesy of the McCormick Research Center, First Division Museum.)

Troops of the 28th Infantry rest on the road during a Franco-American advance near Soissons, Berzy le Sec, near Picady in northern France, on July 16, 1918. (Courtesy of the McCormick Research Center, First Division Museum.)

The capture and occupation of Cantigny and the Picady sector resulted in many German soldiers being captured or forced to surrender. The German prisoners in the picture are being led to 1st Division headquarters in La Coutures, France, on July 16, 1918. (Courtesy of the McCormick Research Center, First Division Museum.)

One of the casualties of the 28th Infantry, Capt. Clarence R. Oliver was killed in action near Plouisy, France, July 19, 1918. (Courtesy of the McCormick Research Center, First Division Museum.)

Maj. Gen. Joseph Dickerman, the commanding general for the 3rd Army (part of the 33rd Division), reviews the Rhinc flotilla in May 1919. (Courtesy of the McCormick Research Center, First Division Museum, Henry Dunn Scrapbook.)

Staff of the VII Corps, 3rd Army pose with Col. John E. Hemphill in France during 1918. (Courtesy of the McCormick Research Center, First Division Museum, Henry Dunn Scrapbook.)

This photograph was taken of Vaux, France, after the artillery barrage and subsequent capture of Verdun by the French, following many counteroffensives in December 1916. This was one of the longest battles of World War I between the Germans and French, lasting 303 days. The casualties were estimated at 377,231 for the French and 337,000 for the Germans—an average of 70,000 a month. (Courtesy of the McCormick Research Center, First Division Museum, Henry Dunn Scrapbook.)

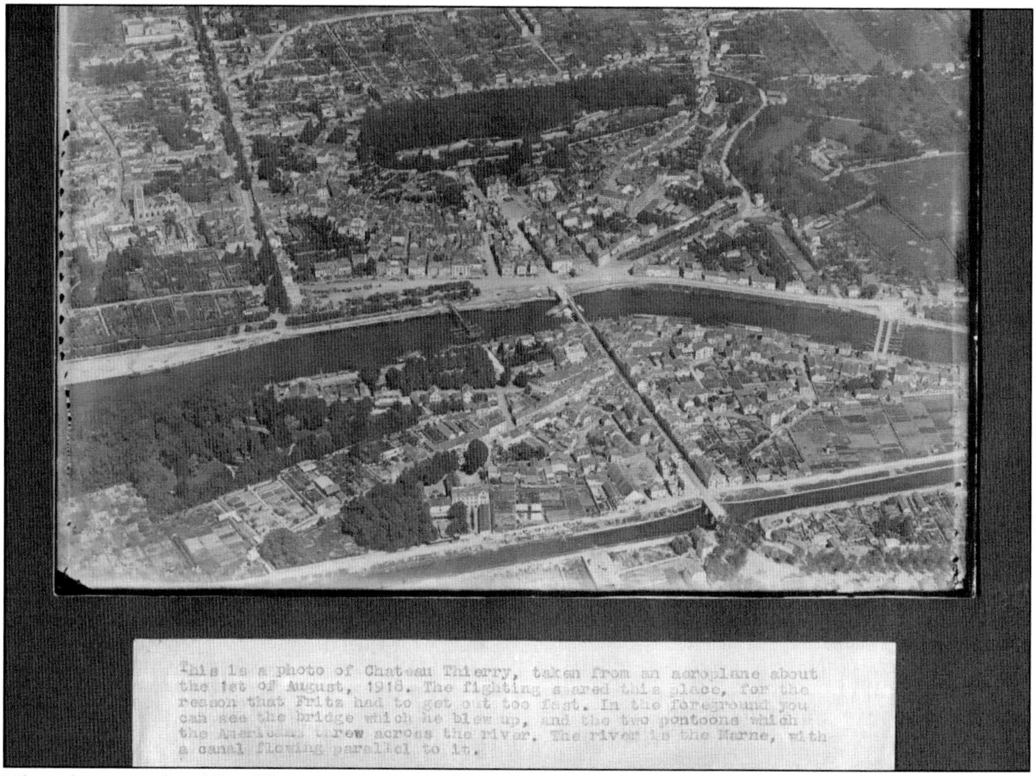

This photograph of the Chateau Thierry taken on August 1, 1918, shows that the estate was spared the ravages of war. The exception was the bridge, blown up by the retreating Germans. The battle was fought on July 18, 1918, under John Pershing, alongside the French and was considered part of the 2nd Battle of the Marne. (Courtesy of the McCormick Research Center, First Division Museum, Henry Dunn Scrapbook.)

This picture shows a review of the 1st Division troops conducted by General Pershing and the French president Georges Clemenceau in August 1917 at Gondrecourt, France. This was taken during the 1st Division engagements in World War I. (Courtesy of the McCormick Research Center, First Division Museum, Henry Dunn Scrapbook.)

The 1st Division troops trained in Gondrecourt, France, during July and August 1917. Training included using the Mle Hotchkiss Machine Gun. The Hotchkiss machine gun was a caliber 8-millimeter with a rate of fire of 450–600 rounds per minute. (Courtesy of the McCormick Research Center, First Division Museum, Henry Dunn Scrapbook.)

The use of aircraft, including air balloons, greatly increased the casualty rates on both sides with their ongoing bombing raids and ability to quickly locate troops on the ground. (Courtesy of the McCormick Research Center, First Division Museum, Henry Dunn Scrapbook.)

During the Battle of Somme in June 1916, German soldiers advance with light machine guns through the ruins of war. (Courtesy of the McCormick Research Center, First Division Museum, Henry Dunn Scrapbook.)

This picture shows evidence of a mustard gas attack in the foreground after trench warfare with the Germans took place in Somme in 1916. (Courtesy of the McCormick Research Center, First Division Museum, Henry Dunn Scrapbook.)

A battle scene near Russia in 1917 depicts the German occupation of a town and the taking of prisoners. (Courtesy of the McCormick Research Center, First Division Museum, Henry Dunn Scrapbook.)

Damaged Italian aircraft are stacked on top of one another in France in 1918. The Italian Caproni was a three-engine heavy bomber that had a crew of four. It could reach a speed of 99 miles per hour. Both the Italians (Allied Powers) and Germans (Central Powers) had ample aircraft, including fighters, bombers, and reconnaissance planes, in World War I. (Courtesy of the McCormick Research Center, First Division Museum, Henry Dunn Scrapbook.)

General Pershing and Maj. Gen. Charles P. Summerall inspect the 1st Battalion, 16th Infantry, 1st Division at Vertuney, France, in September 17, 1918. Summerall commanded the 67th Field Artillery Brigade and the 1st Field Artillery Brigade in operations in France in 1917. Brig. Gen. Theodore Roosevelt Jr. wrote to George C. Marshall stating of General Summerall that he was the biggest troop leader in the US Army. (Courtesy of the McCormick Research Center, First Division Museum.)

Tank 2367 of Company C, 327th Battalion was involved from opening day of the Saint-Mihiel Operation on September 12, 1918. Second Lt. Joseph R. Younglove was in command. This tank operated under the 1st Brigade Tank Corps of the American I Army Corps. (Courtesy of the McCormick Research Center, First Division Museum.)

The 1st Division in the Battle of Saint-Mihiel was joined by the 26th Division in an advance on the occupied town of Montsec, Meuse, France, on September 12, 1918. (Courtesy of the McCormick Research Center, First Division Museum.)

This photograph depicts an advance by the 1st Division on horseback and foot through the town of Essay, France, on September 13, 1918. Notice the medical truck in the foreground. (Courtesy of the McCormick Research Center, First Division Museum.)

Scouts of the 18th Infantry, 1st Division seek cover during the shelling of the town of Exermont, France, on October 7, 1918. (Courtesy of the McCormick Research Center, First Division Museum.)

In this photograph, 1st Division officers study plans in front of the division headquarters. From left to right are Maj. T.R. Cowenlook, Lt. G.B. Conter, and Capt. D.E. Achers in Meuse, France, on October 29, 1918. (Courtesy of the McCormick Research Center, First Division Museum.)

Maj. Gen. Charles P. Summerall leads the troops of the 18th Infantry before their advance through the Argonne Forest, Meuse, France, on October 29, 1918. (Courtesy of the McCormick Research Center, First Division Museum.)

Maj. Gen. Frank Parker, commanding general, poses at the 1st Division headquarters at Verrier en Hesse Farm, Meuse, France, on October 29, 1918. (Courtesy of the McCormick Research Center, First Division Museum.)

Lt. Col. Theodore Roosevelt Jr. is shown with his wife, Eleanor, in war-torn Romagne Meuse, France, on November 13, 1918. Lieutenant Colonel Roosevelt was one of two sons of former president Theodore Roosevelt serving in World War I who had also served in the Spanish-American War. Quentin Roosevelt, a pilot in the US Air Service in World War I, was the fourth son of Theodore Roosevelt and was shot down by a German Fokker plane over the Marne River in France on July 14, 1918. (Courtesy of the McCormick Research Center, First Division Museum.)

Lt. Col. Theodore Roosevelt Jr. (center) is pictured with his wife, Eleanor Butler Roosevelt, and Brig. Gen. Frank Parker in Meuse, France, November 13, 1918. (Courtesy of the McCormick Research Center, First Division Museum.)

The crossing and review of the Armistice Line at Étain, Meuse, France, by the 26th Regiment Infantry on November 11, 1918, is documented in this photograph. From left to right are Brig. Gen. Frank Parker, Brig. Gen. Francis Marshall, Lt. Col. Theodore Roosevelt Jr., Capt. H.M. Leno, and Maj. Thomas Gowenlock. (Courtesy of the McCormick Research Center, First Division Museum.)

Infantries of the 1st Division and elements of the 33rd Division pose in front of the 1st Division Headquarters in Landes Meurthe et Moselle, France, on November 18, 1918. (Courtesy of the McCormick Research Center, First Division Museum.)

Maj. R.K. Whiteson (center) and Pvt. A.M. Hause (right) were decorated with the Distinguished Silver Cross for great heroism at Soissons on July 18, 1918. These men captured a machine gun nest in the way of their advance. Brigadier Gen. William Wright Harts awarded the medals. (Courtesy of the McCormick Research Center, First Division Museum.)

Pvt. A.M. Hause, 28th Infantry, was decorated in Paris, France, by Brigadier General Harts for bravery at the Battle of Soissons on November 24, 1918. (Courtesy of the McCormick Research Center, First Division Museum.)

Capt. N.A. Bourour represented the 28th Regiment Infantry of the 1st Division as the first American to enter Germany from Luxembourg on November 30, 1918. (Courtesy of the McCormick Research Center, First Division Museum.)

Elements of the 1st Division are depicted as various infantries cross over the Moselle River into Wincheringen, Germany, on November 30, 1918. (Courtesy of the McCormick Research Center, First Division Museum.)

American troops, including the 1st Division and elements of the 33rd Division entered Wincheringen, Germany, on November 30, 1918. (Courtesy of the McCormick Research Center, First Division Museum.)

Brig. Gen. F.C. Marshall and staff review the 28th Infantry as it passes over the bridge between Wormeldange and Luxembourg City on November 30, 1918. Identified from left to right are Captain Lanban, Captain Lane (French), Brig. Gen. F.C. Marshall, and Maj. W.C. Livesay. (Courtesy of the McCormick Research Center, First Division Museum.)

The 28th Regiment Infantry, 3rd Brigade, marches along the roadside near the Burg Arras, near Alf, Mosel, Germany. The soldiers were welcomed by children waving at the Americans on December 6, 1918. (Courtesy of the McCormick Research Center, First Division Museum.)

The 1st Division Christmas celebration took place in front of Kaiser Wilhelm's statue in Montabaur, Germany. Partaking in the Christmas celebration on December 25, 1918 were William A. Turner, staff captain of the Salvation Army, as Santa Claus distributing candy, tobacco, and other gifts from families in the United States. (Courtesy of the McCormick Research Center, First Division Museum.)

Maj. Gen. McGlachlin, commander of the 1st Division, pins the Croix de Guerre on the regimental colors of the 28th Infantry. The honor was conferred by Marshall Pétain to the regiment for being the "first American unit to advance at Cantigny." The division was honored at Montabaur, Germany, on January 11, 1919. (Courtesy of the McCormick Research Center, First Division Museum.)

Machine Gun Company K, 28th Regiment Infantry waits in position guarding the neutral zone at the American bridgehead boundary line in Molsberg, Germany, on January 17, 1919. (Courtesy of the McCormick Research Center, First Division Museum.)

Commander in chief Gen. George C. Marshall inspects the troops of the 1st Division near Montabaur, Rhenish Prussia, Germany, on March 14, 1919. (Courtesy of the McCormick Research Center, First Division Museum.)

This monument, called Monument Hill 240, honors the men of the 1st Division who died in the advance on Cantigny in May 1918. It was mainly constructed by the troops of the 1st Division. (Courtesy of the McCormick Research Center, First Division Museum.)

Men of the 1st Division at Cantigny pose for a picture before taking time to decorate the graves of their fallen brethren on May 28, 1919. (Courtesy of the McCormick Research Center, First Division Museum.)

A memorial erected on May 28, 1919, by the French people and the 1st Division stood at an American cemetery in Bolvillers, France, in honor of the fallen nearly a year after the first major engagement at Cantigny. (Courtesy of the McCormick Research Center, First Division Museum.)

German children, adults, and soldiers watch and enjoy the US Army 1st Division circus through small holes in a tent in Montabaur, Rhenish Prussia, Germany, on July 11, 1919. (Courtesy of the McCormick Research Center, First Division Museum.)

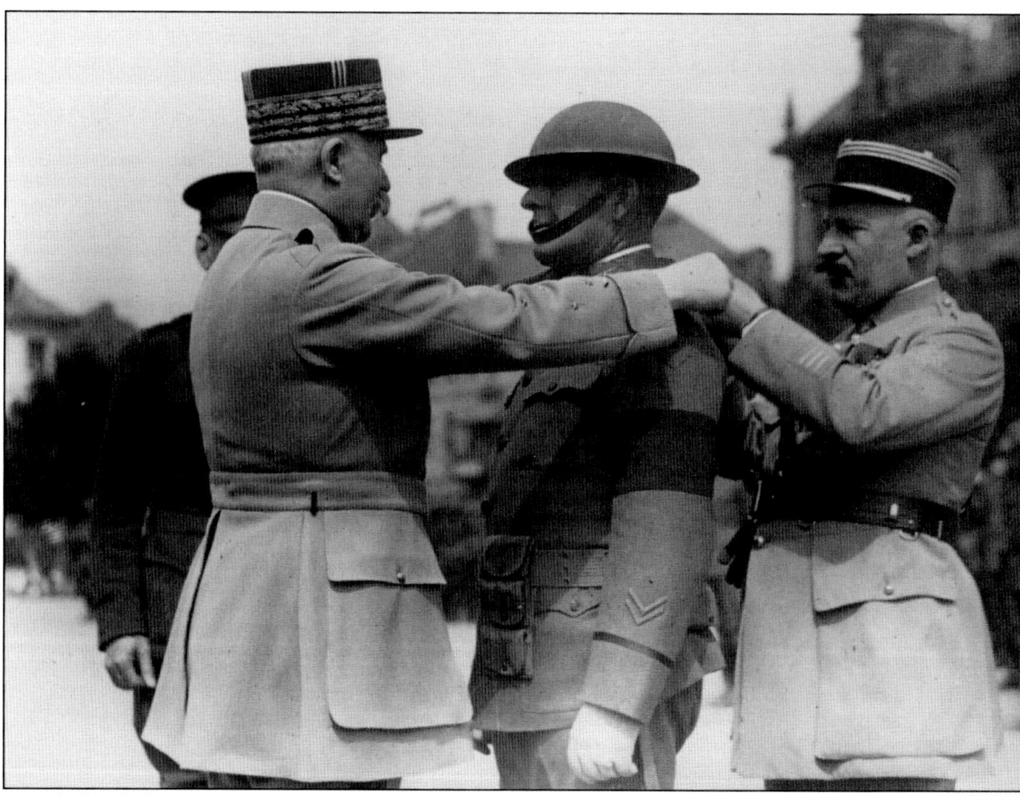

Marshall Philippe Pétain decorates Maj. Gen. Edward T. McGlachlin, who commanded the 1st Division. He was made a Commander of the Legion of Honor near Coblens in Rhenish, Prussia, on July 18, 1919. (Courtesy of the McCormick Research Center, First Division Museum.)

Gen. John J. Pershing and Major General Allen speak to the commander of the 1st Division after review, near Coblens in Rhenish Prussia, on August 1, 1919. (Courtesy of the McCormick Research Center, First Division Museum.)

Maj. Gen. Charles P. Summerall was the division commander of the IV Army Corps, 1st Division, AEF. This photograph was taken after the war. (Courtesy of the McCormick Research Center, First Division Museum.)

Pres. Woodrow Wilson, commander in chief, and Gen. John J. Pershing recognized the 1st Division with a salute during a parade in Washington, DC, during 1919. (Courtesy of the McCormick Research Center, First Division Museum.)

Four

Honoring All the Veterans of World War I from Kane County

For World War I, full casualties of the 33rd Division were 798 KIA, 7,299 WIA, 148 missing, and 18 captured with a total of 8,263. Kane County World War I loses totaled 151 men. Aurora alone lost 85 men during their time in service. But numbers fail to fully grasp the depth of sacrifice not only by Kane County, but also by the entire nation during both world wars. The last Kane County World War I veteran, Raymond Geister, died on February 2, 2000, age of 105. Some examples of gallantry include that of Pvt. Marshall Statton, 129th Infantry, 33rd Division, who survived all engagements but was killed on June 5, 1919, in Luxemburg. Another soldier of the 18th Infantry, 1st Division was Lawrence Conrad, who was gassed on May 3, 1918, returned to the front in September 1918, and was killed in action at Exermont on October 5, 1918. Pvt. John Nagel, 39th Infantry, engaged in battles at Aisne-Marme, Vesle, and Faucon Sectors, Saint-Mihiel, and was killed in action at Meuse-Argonne on September 26, 1918. Wilfred Oakes, corporal, 129th, 33rd Division of St. Charles, was severely wounded on October 14, 1919, and died two days later. He was the first serviceman from St. Charles to die in action, his family being notified in November, 1919. Another soldier who died in action in the Argonne Woods battle toward the end of the war, on October 5, 1918, was Pvt. Henry Guy Shaw, Co. D, 129th, 33rd Division.

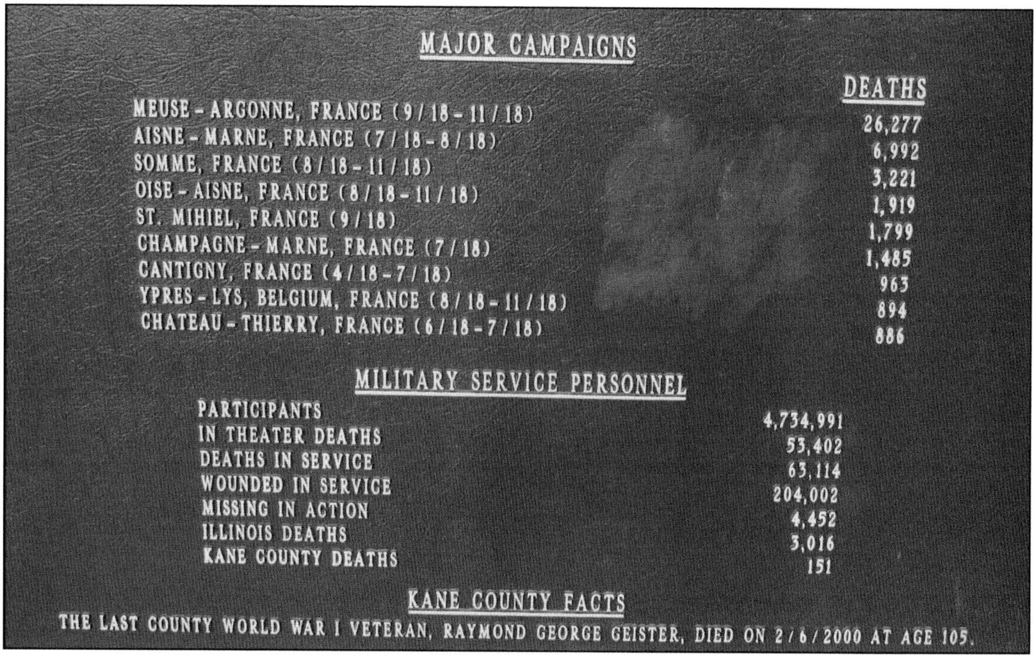

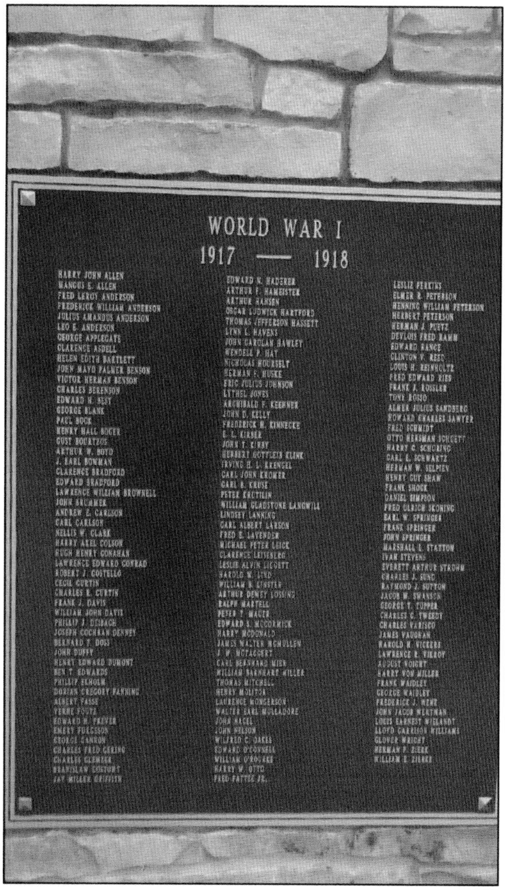

The Kane County Veterans Memorial notes the major campaigns in World War I and statistics of military service personnel nationally for the state of Illinois and Kane County. One hundred fifty-one men from Kane County died in service, including those who died in camp, of sickness, as a result of wounds, or were killed in battle. (Both, author's collection.)

Aurora Boys Who Paid *the* Supreme Sacrifice

Allen, John Harry	Pvt.	H. Q. Co.	16th Inf. 1st Div. Killed in action May 2, 1918.
Anderson, Frederick	Seaman		U. S. Navy. Died of Flu, Oct. 7, 1918.
Asdell, Clarence	Pvt.		161st Depot Brigade. Died.
Berenson, Charles	Pvt.	Bat. B	332nd Field Art. 86th Div. Died September 1, 1918.
Best, Edward H.	Lieut.		115th Engineers. Died of disease.
Blank, George	Pvt.	Co. I	129th Inf. 33rd Div. Killed October 10, 1918.
Bock, Paul	Pvt.	Co. M	103rd Inf. Killed July 21, 1918.
Boger, Henry C. (col.)	Lieut.	Co. D	365th Inf. Killed November 8, 1918.
Bourtzos, Gust	Pvt.	Co. E	353rd Inf. Killed October 29, 1918.
Boyd, Arthur Nelson	Pvt.	M. G. Co.	139th Inf. Co. C. 115th Inf. 42nd Div. Killed September 12, 1918.
Bowman, Earl	Pvt.	Co. I	129th Inf. 33rd Div. Died December 2, 1918.
Brummer, John	Pvt.	Troop L	23rd Cavalry. Died October 26, 1917.
Conrad, Lawrence Edward	Corp.	Co. C	18th Inf. 1st Div. Killed Oct. 7, 1918.
Conahan, Hugh Henry	MAA.		U. S. Navy. Died of Flu, September 25, 1918.
Curtin, Cecil	Pvt.	H. Q. Co.	148th Inf. Killed October 31, 1918.
Curtin, Charles R.	Pvt.	Co. B	5th Limited Service. Died of Flu, October 7, 1918.
Carlson, Carl	Pvt.	Co. H	23rd Inf. Killed October 3, 1918.
Clark, Nellis	Pvt.		108th Engrs. 33rd Div. Killed.
Davis, William John	Pvt.	Co. I	129th Inf. 33rd Div. Killed.
DeHart, Raymond	Pvt.		Engrs. Reserve Corps. Died May 12, 1919.
Deibach, Phillip	Pvt.	H. Q. Co.	Sweeney Auto School. Died August 4, 1918.
Denney, Joseph Cochran	Yeoman 2c.		U. S. Navy. Died December 23, 1917.
Dumont, Henry Edward	Pvt.	Co. M	341st Inf. Killed October 15, 1918.
Fanning, Dorian	Pvt.		50th Anti-aircraft. Died Jan. 4, 1919.
Foutz, Verne	Pvt.	Co. I	129th Inf. 33rd Div. Died April 18, 1918.
Furgeson, Emery	Pvt.		161st Depot Brigade. Died.
Gering, Charles Fred	Pvt.	64th Co.	165th Depot Brig. Died Nov. 6, 1918.
Glemzer, Charles	Pvt.		132nd Inf. 33rd Div. Killed.
Gostowt, Branislaw	Pvt.		132nd Inf. 33rd Div. Killed.
Halverson, Harry	Corp.	Co. A	39th Inf. 4th Div. Killed September 30, 1918.
Hassett, Thomas Jefferson	Pvt. 1c.	M. G. Co.	39th Inf. Died of wounds.
Henn, John P.	Pvt.	Co. K	316th Inf. Killed.
Hoppe, William Henry	Pvt.	Cook and Baker Div.	Camp Custer. Died October 10, 1918.
Hourselt, Nicholas	Pvt.	Co. I	129th Inf. 33rd Div. Killed.
Hupach, Lyle John			
Jones, Lythel	Corp.	Co. D	129th Inf. 33rd Div. Killed.
Kasal, Frank			
Keehner, Arch F.	Pvt.	H. Q. Co.	335th Inf. Died.
Kirby, John T.	Pvt.	Bat. A	7th Field Art. 1st Div. Killed.

[12]

World War I veterans from Aurora who died in service to their country are listed in *With the Colors from Aurora, Illinois, 1917–1919*, with information as to their service, regiments, and the battles they engaged in. As indicated, some of the men survived many battles but sadly died toward the end of the war. Many of the soldiers fought in the 129th Infantry or other infantries of the 33rd Division. (Courtesy of the Aurora History Museum.)

Aurora Boys Who Paid *the* Supreme Sacrifice

Klink, Herbert Gottleib	LMMA.		U. S. Naval Aviation. Died.
Krutilin, Peter	Corp.	Co. A	16th Inf. 1st Div. Killed.
Kirber, E. L.			Killed.
Lanning, Lindsey	Pvt.	Co. I	129th Inf. 33rd Div. Killed.
Langwill, William G.	Major	3rd Batt.	30th Inf. Killed October 10, 1918.
Leick, Michael Peter	Pvt.	Co. M	354th Inf. Died April 10, 1919.
Liggett, Leslie	Ensign		U. S. Navy. Died.
Linster, William	Pvt.	Co. B	108th Engrs. 33rd Div. Died June 23, 1918.
Lossing, Arthur	Pvt. 1c.	Co. A	38th Inf. Died August 25, 1918.
McCormick, Edward	Pvt.	Co. B	5th Limited Service. Died of Flu, October 6, 1918.
McDonald, Harry	Cook	Co. I	129th Inf. 33rd Div. Killed.
McMullen, James Walter	Blks. 2c.		U. S. Navy. Died.
McTaggert, J. W.	Pvt.	Co. H	6th U. S. Marines. Killed.
Martell, Ralph	Pvt.	Co. I	129th Inf. 33rd Div. Killed.
Mauer, Peter	Corp.	Co. I	129th Inf. 33rd Div. Died February 7, 1919.
Miller, Harry Von	Pvt.	Co. A	4th Inf. Air Service. Died.
Mitchell, Thomas	Pvt.	Co. H	129th Inf. 33rd Div. Killed.
Molitor, Henry	Pvt.	Co. C	332nd M. G. Co. Died.
Mulladore, Earl	Pvt.	Supply Co.	129th Inf. 33rd Div. Died.
Nagel, John	Pvt.	Co. I	39th Inf. 4th Div. Killed September 26, 1918.
Nelson, John	Bugler		Killed.
Oakes, Wilfred	Corp.	Co. D	129th Inf. 33rd Div. Killed.
Pattee, Fred	Pvt.	H. Q. Co.	48th Inf. Died of Flu.
Perkins, M. R.	Pvt.		Canadian Highlanders. Killed.
Perkins, Leslie	Pvt.	Co. K	309th Inf. Killed.
Peterson, Henning William	Pvt.	Co. I	131st Inf. 33rd Div. Killed.
Peterson, Herbert	1st Lieut.		Director R. R. and Roads Engrs. Killed.
Puetz, Herman J.			Died.
Ries, Fred Edward	Ensign		U. S. Naval Aviation. Killed.
Rossler, Frank J.	Pvt.	Co. 37	Military Police Div. Killed.
Schwartz, Carl E.	Corp.	Co. B	302nd Water Tank Train. Died.
Shaw, Henry Guy	Pvt.	Co. D	129th Inf. 33rd Div. Killed.
Shock, Frank	Pvt.		Died.
Simpson, Daniel	Corp.	Co. D	129th Inf. 33rd Div. Killed.
Springer, John			Killed.
Springer, Frank			Killed.
Statton, Marshall L.	Pvt.	M. G. Co.	129th Inf. 33rd Div. Died.
Stevens, Ivan	Pvt.	Troop K	17th Cavalry. Died.
Vikroy, Lawrence	Pvt.	Co. M	353rd Inf. 89th Div. Killed.
Wielandt, Louis E.	Cook		29th P. O. D. Died October 15, 1918.
Waidley, George	Pvt.	Co. D	129th Inf. 33rd Div. Died of wounds.
Waidley, Frank	Srgt.	Co. H	318th Inf. Died of wounds.
Wright, Grover	Pvt.		86th Div. Drowned.
Wertman, John Jacob	Pvt.	Co. I	129th Inf., then 167th Inf. Died.
Wenz, Fred	Corp.	Co. C	121st Inf. Died at Camp Upton.
Zille, Louis			

This list indicates at least two families who lost two sons in the war. They were John and Frank Springer and George and Frank Waidley. The list of men who died also indicates that many died while training in various camps or of influenza. (Courtesy of the Aurora History Museum.)

Pictured are Aurora World War I veterans who died in service accompanied by additional information as to their individual training, entrance to service, and the place of their death. (Courtesy of the Aurora History Museum.)

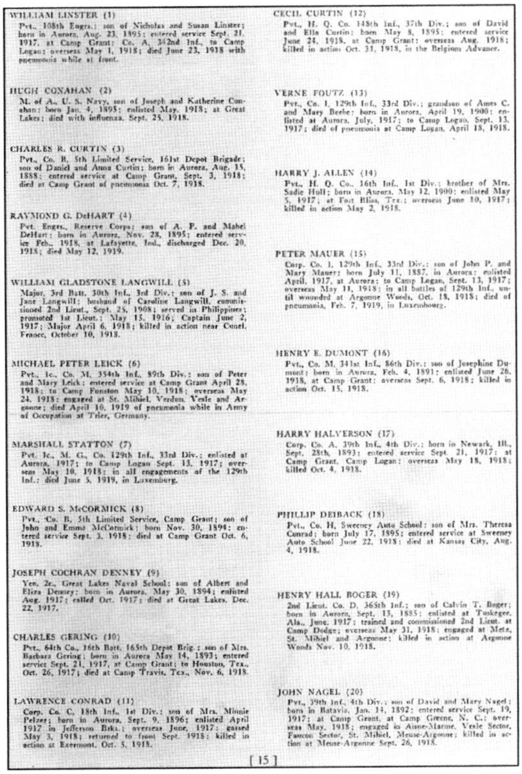

WILLIAM LINSTER (1)
Pvt., 108th Engrs.; son of Nicholas and Susan Linster; born in Aurora, Aug. 23, 1895; entered service Sept. 21, 1917, at Camp Grant; Co. A, 342nd Inf., to Camp Logan; overseas May 1, 1918; died June 23, 1918 with pneumonia while at front.

HUGH CONAHAN (2)
M. of A., U. S. Navy, son of Joseph and Katherine Conahan; born Jan. 4, 1895; enlisted May, 1918; at Great Lakes; died with influenza, Sept. 25, 1918.

CHARLES R. CURTIN (3)
Pvt., Co. B, 5th Limited Service, 161st Depot Brigade; son of Daniel and Anna Curtin; born in Aurora, Aug. 15, 1888; entered service at Camp Grant, Sept. 3, 1918; died at Camp Grant of pneumonia Oct. 7, 1918.

RAYMOND G. DeHART (4)
Pvt. Engrs., Reserve Corps; son of A. P. and Mabel DeHart; born in Aurora, Nov. 28, 1895; entered service Feb., 1918, at Lafayette, Ind., discharged Dec. 20, 1918; died May 12, 1919.

WILLIAM GLADSTONE LANGWILL (5)
Major, 3rd Batt. 30th Inf., 3rd Div.; son of J. S. and Jane Langwill; husband of Caroline Langwill, commissioned 2nd Lieut., Sept. 25, 1908; served in Philippines; promoted 1st Lieut.; May 15, 1916; Captain June 2, 1917; Major April 6, 1918; killed in action near Cunel, France, October 10, 1918.

MICHAEL PETER LEICK (6)
Pvt., 1c., Co. M, 354th Inf., 89th Div.; son of Peter and Mary Leick; entered service at Camp Grant April 28, 1918; to Camp Funston May 10, 1918; overseas May 24, 1918; engaged at St. Mihiel, Verdun, Vesle and Argonne; died April 10, 1919 of pneumonia while in Army of Occupation at Trier, Germany.

MARSHALL STATTON (7)
Pvt. 1c., M. G., Co. 129th Inf., 33rd Div.; enlisted at Aurora, 1917; to Camp Logan Sept. 13, 1917; overseas May 10, 1918; in all engagements of the 129th Inf.; died June 5, 1919, in Luxemburg.

EDWARD S. McCORMICK (8)
Pvt., Co. B, 5th Limited Service, Camp Grant; son of John and Emma McCormick; born Nov. 30, 1894; entered service Sept. 3, 1918; died at Camp Grant Oct. 6, 1918.

JOSEPH COCHRAN DENNEY (9)
Yeo. 2c., Great Lakes Naval School; son of Albert and Eliza Denney; born in Aurora, May 30, 1894; enlisted Aug. 1917; called Oct. 1917; died at Great Lakes, Dec. 22, 1917.

CHARLES GERING (10)
Pvt., 64th Co., 16th Batt. 165th Depot Brig.; son of Mrs. Barbara Gering; born in Aurora May 14, 1893; entered service Sept. 21, 1917, at Camp Grant; to Houston, Tex., Oct. 26, 1917; died at Camp Travis, Tex., Nov. 6, 1918.

LAWRENCE CONRAD (11)
Corp. Co. C, 18th Inf., 1st Div.; son of Mrs. Minnie Pelzer; born in Aurora, Sept. 9, 1896; enlisted April 1917 in Jefferson Brks.; overseas June, 1917; gassed May 3, 1918; returned to front Sept. 1918; killed in action at Exermont, Oct. 5, 1918.

CECIL CURTIN (12)
Pvt., H. Q. Co. 148th Inf., 37th Div.; son of David and Ella Curtin; born May 8, 1895; entered service June 24, 1918, at Camp Grant; overseas Aug. 1918; killed in action Oct. 31, 1918, in the Belgium Advance.

VERNE FOUTZ (13)
Pvt., Co. I, 129th Inf., 33rd Div.; grandson of Ames C. and Mary Beebe; born in Aurora, April 19, 1900; enlisted at Aurora, July, 1917; to Camp Logan, Sept. 13, 1917; died of pneumonia at Camp Logan, April 18, 1918.

HARRY J. ALLEN (14)
Pvt., H. Q. Co., 16th Inf., 1st Div.; brother of Mrs. Sadie Hull; born in Aurora, May 12, 1900; enlisted May 5, 1917; at Fort Bliss, Tex.; overseas June 10, 1917; killed in action May 2, 1918.

PETER MAUER (15)
Corp. Co. I, 129th Inf., 33rd Div.; son of John P. and Mary Mauer; born July 11, 1887, in Aurora; enlisted April, 1917, at Aurora; to Camp Logan, Sept. 13, 1917; overseas May 11, 1918; in all battles of 129th Inf., until wounded at Argonne Woods, Oct. 18, 1918; died of pneumonia, Feb. 7, 1919, in Luxembourg.

HENRY E. DUMONT (16)
Pvt., Co. M, 341st Inf., 86th Div.; son of Josephine Dumont; born in Aurora, Feb. 4, 1891; enlisted June 26, 1918, at Camp Grant; overseas Sept. 6, 1918; killed in action Oct. 15, 1918.

HARRY HALVERSON (17)
Corp. Co. A, 39th Inf., 4th Div.; born in Newark, Ill., Sept. 28th, 1893; entered service Sept. 21, 1917; at Camp Grant, Camp Logan; overseas May 18, 1918; killed Oct. 4, 1918.

PHILLIP DEIBACK (18)
Pvt., Co. H, Sweeney Auto School; son of Mrs. Theresa Conrad; born July 17, 1895; entered service at Sweeney Auto School June 22, 1918; died at Kansas City, Aug. 4, 1918.

HENRY HALL BOGER (19)
2nd Lieut. Co. D, 365th Inf.; son of Calvin T. Boger; born in Aurora, Sept. 13, 1885; enlisted at Tuskegee, Ala., June, 1917; trained and commissioned 2nd Lieut. at Camp Dodge; overseas May 31, 1918; engaged at Metz, St. Mihiel and Argonne; killed in action at Argonne Woods Nov. 10, 1918.

JOHN NAGEL (20)
Pvt., 39th Inf., 4th Div.; son of David and Mary Nagel; born in Batavia, Jan. 14, 1892; entered service Sept. 19, 1917; at Camp Grant, at Camp Greene, N. C.; overseas May, 1918; engaged in Aisne-Marne, Vesle Sector, Faucon Sector, St. Mihiel, Meuse-Argonne; killed in action at Meuse-Argonne Sept. 26, 1918.

[15]

As indicated, many soldiers died of wounds well after the cessation of war in November 1918, such as Raymond G. DeHart, Michael Peter Leick, Marshall Stratton, and Peter Mauer, Additionally, some died during the last major engagement at Meuse-Argonne from September through November 1918. Some never made it overseas, dying either at Camp Grant, Camp Logan, Camp Travis, or at the Great Lakes Training center. (Courtesy of the Aurora History Museum.)

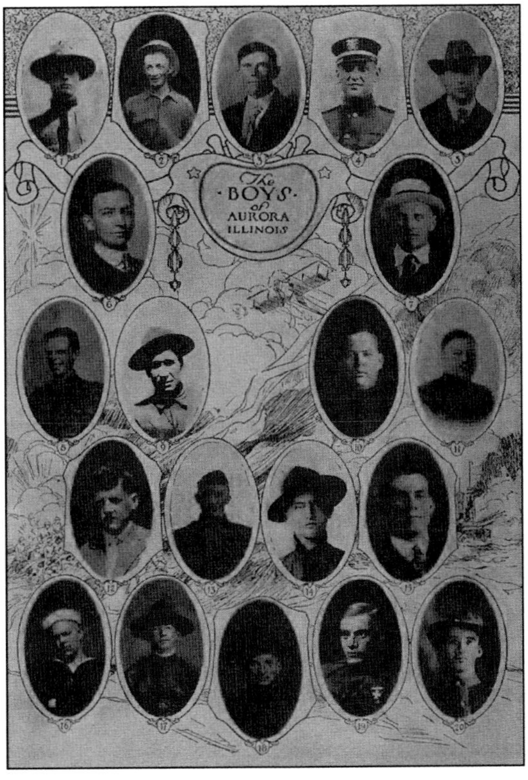

Pvt. Dorian Gregory Fanning (No. 1) served in Medical Corps 5th Anti-Aircraft of Sandwich, Illinois. He was wounded and in a hospital at Brest when he was sent home. Unfortunately, he never made it home. Private Fanning died on the USS *President Grant* traveling back to the United States on January 4, 1919. (Courtesy of the Aurora History Museum.)

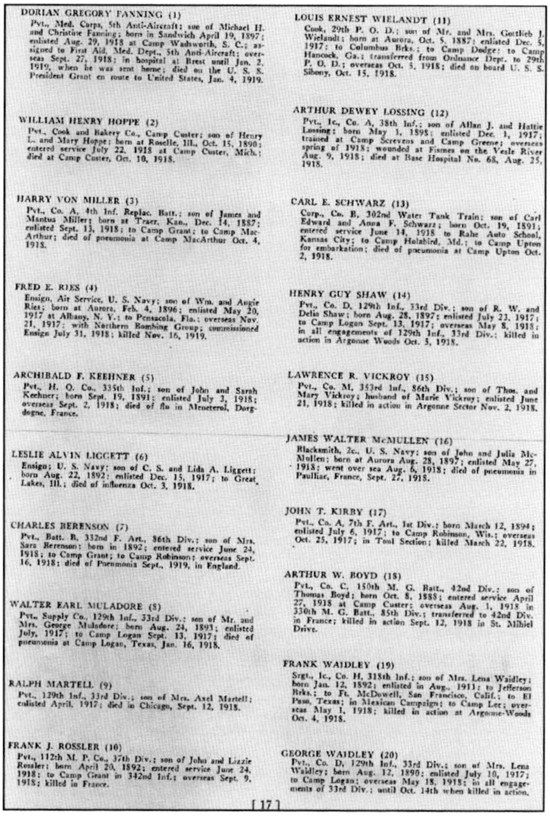
DORIAN GREGORY FANNING (1)
Pvt., Med. Corps, 5th Anti-Aircraft; son of Michael H. and Christine Fanning; born in Sandwich April 19, 1897; enlisted Aug. 29, 1918 at Camp Wadsworth, S. C.; assigned to First Aid, Med. Dept., 5th Anti-Aircraft; overseas Sept. 27, 1918; in hospital at Brest until Jan. 2, 1919, when he was sent home; died on the U. S. S. President Grant en route to United States, Jan. 4, 1919.

WILLIAM HENRY HOPPE (2)
Pvt., Cook and Bakery Co., Camp Custer; son of Henry L. and Mary Hoppe; born at Roselle, Ill., Oct. 15, 1890; entered service July 22, 1918 at Camp Custer, Mich.; died at Camp Custer, Oct. 10, 1918.

HARRY VON MILLER (3)
Pvt., Co. A, 4th Inf. Replac. Batt.; son of James and Mantua Miller; born at Traer, Kan., Dec. 14, 1887; enlisted Sept. 13, 1918; to Camp Grant; to Camp MacArthur; died of pneumonia at Camp MacArthur Oct. 4, 1918.

FRED E. RIES (4)
Ensign, Air Service, U. S. Navy; son of Wm. and Angie Ries; born at Aurora, Feb. 4, 1896; enlisted May 20, 1917 at Albany, N. Y.; to Pensacola, Fla.; overseas Nov. 21, 1917; with Northern Bombing Group; commissioned Ensign July 31, 1918; killed Nov. 16, 1919.

ARCHIBALD F. KEEHNER (5)
Pvt., H. Q. Co., 335th Inf.; son of John and Sarah Keehner; born Sept. 19, 1891; enlisted July 3, 1918; overseas Sept. 2, 1918; died of flu in Meneterol, Dorgdogne, France.

LESLIE ALVIN LIGGETT (6)
Ensign; U. S. Navy; son of C. S. and Lida A. Liggett; born Aug. 22, 1892; enlisted Dec. 15, 1917; to Great Lakes, Ill.; died of influenza Oct. 3, 1918.

CHARLES BERENSON (7)
Pvt., Batt. B, 332nd F. Art., 86th Div.; son of Mrs. Sara Berenson; born in 1892; entered service June 24, 1918; to Camp Grant; to Camp Robinson; overseas Sept. 16, 1918; died of Pneumonia Sept., 1919, in England.

WALTER EARL MULADORE (8)
Pvt., Supply Co., 129th Inf., 33rd Div.; son of Mr. and Mrs. George Muladore; born Aug. 24, 1893; enlisted July, 1917; to Camp Logan Sept. 13, 1917; died of pneumonia at Camp Logan, Texas, Jan. 16, 1918.

RALPH MARTELL (9)
Pvt., 129th Inf., 33rd Div.; son of Mrs. Axel Martell; enlisted April, 1917; died in Chicago, Sept. 12, 1918.

FRANK J. ROSSLER (10)
Pvt., 112th M. P. Co., 37th Div.; son of John and Lizzie Rossler; born April 20, 1892; entered service June 24, 1918; to Camp Grant in 342nd Inf.; overseas Sept. 9, 1918; killed in France.

LOUIS ERNEST WIELANDT (11)
Cook, 29th P. O. D.; son of Mr. and Mrs. Gottlieb J. Wielandt; born at Aurora, Oct. 5, 1887; enlisted Dec. 5, 1917; to Columbus Brks.; to Camp Dodge; to Camp Hancock, Ga.; transferred from Ordnance Dept. to 29th P. O. D.; overseas Oct. 5, 1918; died on board U. S. S. Sibony, Oct. 15, 1918.

ARTHUR DEWEY LOSSING (12)
Pvt., 1c, Co. A, 38th Inf.; son of Allan J. and Hattie Lossing; born May 1, 1898; enlisted Dec. 1, 1917; trained at Camp Screvens and Camp Greene; overseas spring of 1918; wounded at Fismes on the Vesle River Aug. 9, 1918; died at Base Hospital No. 68, Aug. 25, 1918.

CARL E. SCHWARZ (13)
Corp., Co. B, 302nd Water Tank Train; son of Carl Edward and Anna F. Schwarz; born Oct. 19, 1891; entered service June 14, 1918 to Rahe Auto School, Kansas City; to Camp Holabird, Md.; to Camp Upton for embarkation; died of pneumonia at Camp Upton Oct. 2, 1918.

HENRY GUY SHAW (14)
Pvt., Co. D, 129th Inf., 33rd Div.; son of R. W. and Delia Shaw; born Aug. 28, 1897; enlisted July 23, 1917; to Camp Logan Sept. 13, 1917; overseas May 8, 1918; in all engagements of 129th Inf., 33rd Div.; killed in action in Argonne Woods Oct. 5, 1918.

LAWRENCE R. VICKROY (15)
Pvt., Co. M, 353rd Inf., 86th Div.; son of Thos. and Mary Vickroy; husband of Marie Vickroy; enlisted June 21, 1918; killed in action in Argonne Sector Nov. 2, 1918.

JAMES WALTER McMULLEN (16)
Blacksmith, 2c., U. S. Navy; son of John and Julia McMullen; born at Aurora Aug. 28, 1897; enlisted May 27, 1918; went over sea Aug. 6, 1918; died of pneumonia in Paulliac, France, Sept. 27, 1918.

JOHN T. KIRBY (17)
Pvt., Co. A, 7th F. Art., 1st Div.; born March 12, 1894; enlisted July 6, 1917; to Camp Robinson, Wis.; overseas Oct. 25, 1917; in Toul Section; killed March 22, 1918.

ARTHUR W. BOYD (18)
Pvt., Co. C, 150th M. G. Batt., 42nd Div.; son of Thomas Boyd; born Oct. 8, 1888; entered service April 27, 1918 at Camp Custer; overseas Aug. 1, 1918 in 330th M. G. Batt., 85th Div.; transferred to 42nd Div. in France; killed in action Sept. 12, 1918 in St. Mihiel Drive.

FRANK WAIDLEY (19)
Srgt., 1c., Co. H, 318th Inf.; son of Mrs. Lena Waidley; born Jan. 12, 1892; enlisted in Aug., 1911; to Jefferson Brks.; to Ft. McDowell, San Francisco, Calif.; to El Paso, Texas; in Mexican Campaign; to Camp Lee; overseas May 1, 1918; killed in action at Argonne-Woods Oct. 4, 1918.

GEORGE WAIDLEY (20)
Pvt., Co. D, 129th Inf., 33rd Div.; son of Mrs. Lena Waidley; born Aug. 12, 1890; enlisted July 10, 1917; to Camp Logan; overseas May 18, 1918; in all engagements of 33rd Div.; until Oct. 14th when killed in action.

[17]

Many of the men died in camp of influenza or pneumonia, never to engage in battle. Fred Ries was killed on November 16, 1919, as part of the Northern Bombing Group. Frank Waidley served in the Mexican Campaign and died at Argonne Woods on October 4, 1918, just 10 days before his brother George was killed in action having been a part of all the engagements of the 33rd Division. (Courtesy of the Aurora History Museum.)

Karl Gartner, of Co. D, 132 Infantry Division of St. Charles, trained at Camp Grant. He wrote to his family on July 30, 1918, that "as we were going out of the trench, he, Jerry (Germany) was above us with planes and dropped about four bombs about a 100 yards away from us. I later saw Jay Doherty of the 108th Engineers and Jack Gaffney of Co. K." (Courtesy of the St. Charles History Center.)

Somewhere near the front in France during August 1918, Pvt. Jack Gaffney, Co. K, 33rd Division, Illinois National Guard stands near his mess tent with a pennant noting his hometown of Elburn, Illinois. (Author's collection.)

Pvt. Jack Gaffney, brother of the author's grandfather Joseph C. Gaffney, is pictured with three of his colleagues in the trench, 33rd Division, Illinois National Guard, somewhere near the front in France in August, 1918. (Author's collection.)

TANK pris aux BOCHES près

This was a typical battle scene: a German tank making its way through a trench area and through barbed wire during the battle of Reims in France. Tank warfare was introduced in World War I, making a substantial impact in the history of warfare. (Courtesy of the Aurora History Museum.)

A soldier's view of the 132nd Infantry, 33rd Division readying for battle in a frontline trench in France on September 1918 is captured in this image. Many of these men of the 33rd Division had previously fought valiantly and helped the newer soldiers along as the war was nearing its end. (Courtesy of the Aurora History Museum.)

French soldiers and citizenry assisted with the burying of Allied soldiers following battles in July 1918 near Reims, France. (Courtesy of the Aurora History Museum.)

This woman from Kane County served with others from Aurora and Oswego in the Daughters of the American Revolution as well as the Women's Naval Service in World War I. Below, women serve overseas in France during World War I. (Both, courtesy of the Aurora History Museum.)

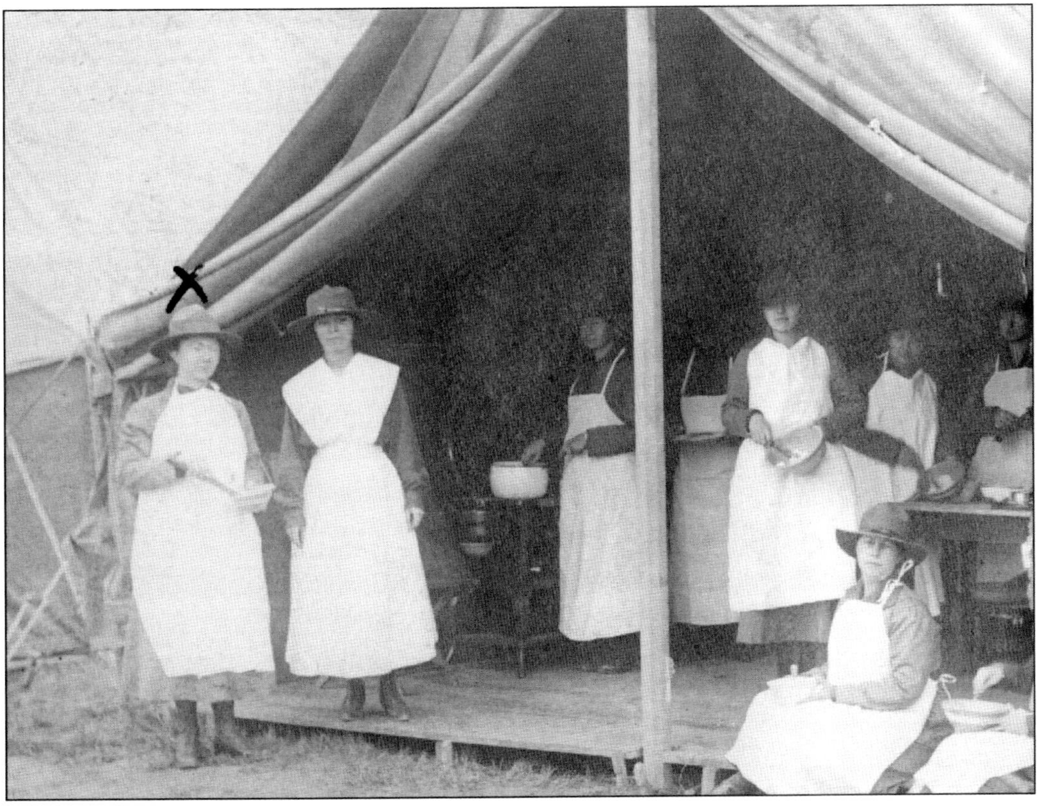

A mobile dressing station makes its way through a battle zone; the unit was tasked with finding wounded service personnel in Béthencourt, France, during the Meuse-Argonne offensive from October 9–21, 1918. (Courtesy of the Elgin Historical Society.)

Pictured is a desolate and snow-covered scene of a recent battle in Béthencourt, Somme Valley, during November 1918. (Courtesy of the Elgin Historical Society.)

Second Lieutenant Wilkening of Elgin, Illinois, poses with his horse while serving somewhere in France in 1918 with the 33rd Division. (Courtesy of the Elgin Historical Society.)

These soldiers from Elgin, serving with the 33rd Division in France in August 1918, were photographed together on a cobblestone sidewalk. From left to right are (first row) Swede Carlson and Judge Farrell; (second row) ? Hoknner, ? Petschow, Roy Andersen, and unidentified. (Courtesy of the Elgin Historical Society.)

Many soldiers of the 131st Infantry Regiment, 33rd Division were from Kane County, Illinois. This group celebrated victory in World War I at Metz, France, on December 8, 1918. The 131st is shown

presenting its colors at an armistice ceremony. (Courtesy of the Elgin Historical Society.)

This postcard depicted a general view of Camp Grant in Rockford, Illinois, during July 1917. Construction on Camp Grant began on June 24, 1917, with an earlier purchase 3,000 acres of farmland for $835,000 by the government. (Courtesy of Camp Grant Museum.)

Elements of the 33rd Division, Illinois National Guard trained and fired field guns at Camp Grant in 1917. Many of these guns were purchased and provided to the 33rd Division by private funds as well as the government. (Courtesy of Camp Grant Museum.)

Five

World War II

The enormity of the human loss in World War II of personnel nationally, statewide, and in Kane County is evidence by the following numbers: 16,112,566 military service personnel participants; total Pacific and European Theater deaths of 291,557; wounded in service 671,846; missing in action 78,773; Illinois deaths totaling 22,283; Illinois missing in action 1,310; and Kane County deaths totaling 565 military service personnel. Many service personnel from Kane County fought in Europe and the Pacific Theatres in all the armed services. On December 7, 1941, seven from Kane County lost their lives at Pearl Harbor. The list of the lost from Kane County reflects the country as a whole regarding service and sacrifice. The following reflects what many of the men from Kane County as well as nationally encountered on any given day in battle, let alone on June 6, 1944.

An after-action report from June 23, 1944, by the commanding officer, 16th Infantry (1st Division) states regarding the initial June 6th invasion wave of 3rd Battalion, "At 0700 hours all naval shelling had ceased, the air corps had failed to knock out any beach defenses, and there was no supporting fire on the beach defenses where the battalion landed. . . The assault landing craft touched down in front of several rows of underwater obstacles. The personnel waded and struggled ashore by crossing 200 years of open beach under intense enemy file-machine gun, rifle, mortar, artillery, and anti-tank weapons. Many men were hit and injured while still in the water. The company (L), losses at this stage were high—4th section was missing, 1st section leading craft was hit by artillery fire and 19 men of that section were missing."

The initial training of landing operations were performed by elements of the 1st Division in New River, North Carolina, in August 1941. (Courtesy of the McCormick Research Center, First Division Museum.)

The 1st Division Signal Corps training included the handling of a 60-millimeter mortar at Camp Blanding, Florida, pre–World War II. (Courtesy of the McCormick Research Center, First Division Museum.)

The Landing Craft Infantry invasion training disembarked in Algeria, North Africa, with Lt. Gen. Mark Clark in command on June 5, 1943. (Courtesy of the McCormick Research Center, First Division Museum.)

This 1st US Infantry Division symbol was a collaboration of the soldiers and officers of the 1st Division at Fort Benning, Georgia, in April 1940. (Courtesy of the McCormick Research Center, First Division Museum.)

Americans of the 1st Army and 1st Division entered Oran, Algeria, on November 18, 1942. (Courtesy of the McCormick Research Center, First Division Museum.)

Soldiers of the 1st Army and 1st Division enter Oran, Algeria, in an armored vehicle while the soldiers on the side take a break before pushing onward on November 18, 1942. (Courtesy of the McCormick Research Center, First Division Museum.)

Italian prisoners were captured by the 1st Division, led by Maj. Gen. Terry Allen at El Guettar in Tunisia on March 26, 1943. (Courtesy of the McCormick Research Center, First Division Museum.)

From left to right, Maj. Gen. Terry Allen, unidentified, Lt. Col. Lord Grenfell (back to camera), Brig. Gen. Theodore Roosevelt Jr., and Lt. Gen. Omar Bradley hold a meeting of the minds regarding military strategy at Djebel Touta Pass on April 30, 1943. (Courtesy of the McCormick Research Center, First Division Museum.)

This photograph shows an Italian plane shot down near the Tine River, Moustrop, during the Tunisia campaign in North Africa in May 1943. (Courtesy of the McCormick Research Center, First Division Museum.)

The 1st Division and First Army entered Tunisia after the fall season. Note the ruins were a result of the battle between the German and American forces in June 1943. (Courtesy of the McCormick Research Center, First Division Museum.)

The Allied invasion of Sicily and Operation Husky included the seizing of the beaches and surrounding areas at Licata, Sicily, in July 1943. (Courtesy of the McCormick Research Center, First Division Museum.)

The Americans and the British landed under heavy fire in July 1943. The fighting persisted for 38 days while the Allies, including elements of the First Army and 1st Division, drove the German and Italian troops from Sicily. Eventually, they prepared for an assault on the Italian mainland. (Courtesy of the McCormick Research Center, First Division Museum.)

The 1st Division, with elements of the First Army under Gen. George S. Patton along with US Navy support, engaged the Germans and Italians in an amphibious attack of Gela from July 10 to July 12, 1943. The casualties and loses for the United States totaled nearly 2,800. The result was an Allied victory. (Courtesy of the McCormick Research Center, First Division Museum.)

This photograph shows a US Navy ship hit by an Axis plane, probably a Luftwaffe aircraft. The United States invasion fleet did not include any aircraft carriers. The Gela invasion beaches were defended by the Italian XVIII Costal Brigade. Concrete pillboxes, barbed wire, and antitank guns awaited the Allied troops. The 18th Regiment of the 1st Division landed in support. (Courtesy of the McCormick Research Center, First Division Museum.)

The US fleet was under bombardment as the landing craft approached the shore in Gela, Sicily. (Courtesy of the McCormick Research Center, First Division Museum.)

The 18th Regiment of the 1st Division landed in support of troops as they pushed inland toward Gela. The men landing in this photograph are not a part of the first wave, as the beach had already been secured on July 12, 1943. (Courtesy of the McCormick Research Center, First Division Museum.)

This photograph shows Italian troops caught by the 1st Division at El Guetter, Tunisia, on March 26, 1943. (Courtesy of the McCormick Research Center, First Division Museum.)

Elements of the 894th tank destroyers go through the Kasserine Pass in Tunisia on February 25, 1943. (Courtesy of the McCormick Research Center, First Division Museum.)

This photograph was taken in Prate, Italy, on January 26, 1944. The individuals are, from left to right, Maj. Gen. Geoffrey Keyes, II Corps; Gen. Alphonse Juin, French Expeditionary Corps; and Brig. Gen. Theodore Roosevelt Jr., the chief liaison officer with the French. (Courtesy of the McCormick Research Center, First Division Museum.)

This photograph shows services conducted by a Chaplain Derry aboard the USS *Acorn* (AGC-4) before the invasion of Normandy, France, also known as Operation Overlord or D-day, on June 6, 1944. (Courtesy of the McCormick Research Center, First Division Museum.)

Equipment and men were loaded aboard Landing Craft Tanks at Brixham, England, on June 1, 1944. This photograph was taken before crossing the English Channel for the eventual invasion of northern France on D-day. (Courtesy of the McCormick Research Center, First Division Museum.)

Elements of the 3rd Battalion, Company L assisted in the invasion on June 6, 1944. The Landing Craft Vehicle Personnel (LCVP), or Higgins Boat, approaches Fox Beach as part of the additional invasion force. (Courtesy of the McCormick Research Center, First Division Museum.)

This photograph shows American assault troops of the 3rd Battalion, 16th Infantry Regiment, 1st Division ashore and organized at Chalk Cliff on June 6, 1944. (Courtesy of the McCormick Research Center, First Division Museum.)

The wounded who came ashore on the Higgins Boat as part of Company L, 16th Infantry to Chalk Cliff, or Normandy's White Cliffs, Colleville-sur-Mer were tended by medical personnel before any advance on June 6, 1944. (Courtesy of the McCormick Research Center, First Division Museum.)

The wounded amongst the dead of Company L, 16th Infantry at Chalk Cliff, Colleville-sur-Mer were observed by men advancing inland on June 6, 1944. (Courtesy of the McCormick Research Center, First Division Museum.)

The wounded were tended by medical personnel. Many of the men appeared dazed following the invasion and battle on the beach at Chalk Cliff, Colleville-sur-Mer. (Courtesy of the McCormick Research Center, First Division Museum.)

The living found themselves among the dead in a failed attempt to storm a German-held main strip of Omaha Beach. The price of war was evident, as there were a total of 2,499 casualties, with the 1st Division and 29th Division suffering around 2,000 casualties. (Courtesy of the McCormick Research Center, First Division Museum.)

Men of the 1st Division who made it ashore assisted others with a line to troops trying to navigate the water and shoreline at Omaha Beach on D-day. (Courtesy of the McCormick Research Center, First Division Museum.)

Company L, 16th Infantry survivors of a sunken LCVP, Landing Craft Vehicle Personnel, or Higgins Boat come ashore on Omaha Beach, Cherbourg, France, on June 6, 1944. (Courtesy of the McCormick Research Center, First Division Museum.)

The day after D-day, the beachhead was secured with supplies before the men pushed inland into France. (Courtesy of the McCormick Research Center, First Division Museum.)

Sainte-Mère-Église played a vital role on D-day as units of the 82nd Airborne and 101st Airborne occupied the town. The early landings resulted in heavy casualties. Troops awaited identification and burial for their comrades in battle. (Courtesy of the McCormick Research Center, First Division Museum.)

With Utah Beach occupied by the Allied forces, reinforcements and equipment made their way inland on June 8, 1944. Utah Beach was one of the five sectors of the Allied invasion, led by commanders Gen. J. Lawton Collins and Gen. Theodore Roosevelt Jr. The 1st Division landed 21,000 troops with only 197 casualties in the occupation of Utah Beach. (Courtesy of the McCormick Research Center, First Division Museum.)

Troops relax in front of the J. Philippe café and grocery as the French gladly welcome the Americans after they took Sainte-Mère-Église on June 7, 1944. (Courtesy of the McCormick Research Center, First Division Museum.)

Col. Gerald Kelleher (left) and Maj. Bill Goodwin of the 104th Division honor Brig. Gen. Theodore "Ted" Roosevelt III (aka Jr.) at his gravesite. He died from a heart attack after a heavy day of fighting on July 12, 1944. He is buried at the Omaha Beach American Cemetery in Colleville-sur-Mer, Normandy, next to his brother Quentin Roosevelt. Quentin was a pilot in World War I and shot down by the Germans. (Courtesy of the McCormick Research Center, First Division Museum.)

Joseph King and Pvt. William E. Jackson found an alternative way of travel as the 1st Division continued inland in France on July 8, 1944. (Courtesy of the McCormick Research Center, First Division Museum.)

This photograph shows a 75-millimeter German howitzer turret on Omaha Beach. The howitzer could fire a heavy shell from a relatively short barrel with a high trajectory. Along with the German pillboxes, the heavy guns caused a lot of Allied casualties on D-day. (Courtesy of the McCormick Research Center, First Division Museum.)

An American soldier of the 75th Infantry Division analyzes a pillbox near Aachen, Germany, on September 26, 1944. (Courtesy of the McCormick Research Center, First Division Museum.)

The 1st Division, including 3rd Armored Division troops, marches through the bombed-out town of Juyigny-le-Tertre in Brittany, France, while on alert for German snipers on August 2, 1944. (Courtesy of the McCormick Research Center, First Division Museum.)

American troops are welcomed by the French citizens of Lassay, France, on August 12, 1944. The castle located in Lassay was used as a German command post prior to the invasion at Normandy. (Courtesy of the McCormick Research Center, First Division Museum.)

Soldiers of the 1st Division visit a cemetery that honors deceased World War I soldiers in Soissons, France, on August 12, 1944. (Courtesy of the McCormick Research Center, First Division Museum.)

A beach near Vierville-sur-Mer in France located between Utah and Gold Beaches was heavily defended by the Germans and their 88-millimeter guns on D-day. The beach was occupied by infantries of the 1st Division on September 10, 1944. (Courtesy of the McCormick Research Center, First Division Museum.)

This photograph shows the Americans' arrival in Aachen, Germany. The Germans surrendered on October 24, 1944. (Courtesy of the McCormick Research Center, First Division Museum.)

Allied ships, including the USS *Mulberry*, brought men and supplies for the ongoing invasion of Normandy, France. On the left, a row of scuttled ships made a breakwater for the USS *Mulberry* on November 7, 1944. (Courtesy of the McCormick Research Center, First Division Museum.)

At the headquarters of the 1st Infantry Division in Germany, personnel review the route of the "Fighting 1st" through North Africa, Italy, France, and into Germany. (Courtesy of the McCormick Research Center, First Division Museum.)

On September 23, 1944, Archbishop Francis Spellman leads Mass for American troops for the first time on German soil in Aachen, Germany. (Courtesy of the McCormick Research Center, First Division Museum.)

Infantrymen from Company L enter Aachen fully aware of Nazi snipers. Soldiers secured the town on October 13, 1944. (Courtesy of the McCormick Research Center, First Division Museum.)

Company L and 1st Division fire on German positions as the Americans advance through Aachen, Germany, on October 15, 1944. (Courtesy of the McCormick Research Center, First Division Museum.)

The 26th Infantry division watches tanks roll through Zweifall, Germany, on November 15, 1944. (Courtesy of the McCormick Research Center, First Division Museum.)

These unidentified Japanese American soldiers, part of H Company, fire mortar rounds in France as they advance against the Germans on November 17, 1944. (Courtesy of the McCormick Research Center, First Division Museum.)

The 1st Battalion, 18th Infantry Regiment continues to push forward through Hamich, Germany, toward the front lines on November 20, 1944. (Courtesy of the McCormick Research Center, First Division Museum.)

After Thanksgiving, two unidentified friends use their downtime to listen to a Private Williams of the 1st Division play the organ in a Catholic school in Gereonsweiler on November 27, 1944. (Courtesy of the McCormick Research Center, First Division Museum.)

The destruction of war was evident in Liège, Belgium. A row of flats was destroyed by the dreaded V-1 bomb launched from Germany on November 30, 1944. (Courtesy of the McCormick Research Center, First Division Museum.)

In the midst of battle, a tank of the 745th Tank Battalion was hit by the Germans near Hamich, Germany, on November 23, 1944. (Courtesy of the McCormick Research Center, First Division Museum.)

Infantry of the 26th Regiment, 1st Division moves up to cut off a German counterthrust, which threatened Büllingen, Belgium, on December 17, 1944. (Courtesy of the McCormick Research Center, First Division Museum.)

In an effort to stop the German's advance at the Battle of the Bulge, the Americans, including the 26th Infantry, tried to cut off the attempts by the Germans to gain a foothold in the Losheim Gap and Büllingen areas during December 1944. (Courtesy of the McCormick Research Center, First Division Museum.)

Soldiers of Company F, 18th Infantry patrol the woods in Belgium for German parachutists that dropped behind their lines during the Battle of the Bulge on December 18, 1944. (Courtesy of the McCormick Research Center, First Division Museum.)

Soldiers of Company M, 3rd Battalion, 18th Infantry patrol and search for any German paratroopers in Sourbrodt, Belgium, on December 19, 1944. (Courtesy of the McCormick Research Center, First Division Museum.)

Sgt. Ralph B. Nunn of Company M, 18th Infantry spots a German soldier and readies his M1 Garand rifle in response on December 19, 1944. (Courtesy of the McCormick Research Center, First Division Museum.)

Pfc. Clyde F. Terry (left), Headquarters Battery, 5th Field Artillery Battalion, and 1st Lt. Ernest C. Capell, Headquarters 32nd Field Artillery Battalion, prepare for a check flight in a US Army liaison plane near Sourbrodt, Belgium, on January 14, 1945. (Courtesy of the McCormick Research Center, First Division Museum.)

An American soldier of Company F, 16th Infantry Regiment defends his position against the advancing Germans in December 1944. Americans fought in harsh and cold conditions during the Battle of the Bulge. (Courtesy of the McCormick Research Center, First Division Museum.)

Two American soldiers wounded near Wavre, Belgium, are being carried in a doodlebug on January 15, 1945. The soldiers are with the 3rd Battalion, 16th Infantry Division. (Courtesy of the McCormick Research Center, First Division Museum.)

Company F of the 16th Infantry Division marches through the Stanis Forest in Germany, near Munich. The troops quickly moved toward Berlin in a race against the Russians to occupy the city on November 16, 1945. (Courtesy of the McCormick Research Center, First Division Museum.)

On February 19, 1945, Brig. Gen. Clift Andres (front), commanding general of the 1st Division, escorts Lt. Gen. Omar Bradley of the 18th Army Group Headquarters. (Courtesy of the McCormick Research Center, First Division Museum.)

Company B of the 16th Infantry Signal Corps crosses the Rur River in Kreuzau, Germany, on February 25, 1945. (Courtesy of the McCormick Research Center, First Division Museum.)

The men of Company B make dangerous advancements near the bridge at the Rhine near Bonn, Germany, on March 9, 1945, in an effort to cross the river. (Courtesy of the McCormick Research Center, First Division Museum.)

Soldiers of the 16th Regiment, 1st Division cross the Weser River in an assault on the German town of Fürstenberg. They captured Wenden from the Germans on April 8, 1945. (Courtesy of the McCormick Research Center, First Division Museum.)

Brig. Gen. George A. Taylor (left) of the 1st Division and Capt. Carl Oslve, interpreter, watch Lt. Gen. Fritz Banicke, who was commanding German forces near Sibogen, sign surrender papers for troops and equipment under his command on March 7, 1945. (Courtesy of the McCormick Research Center, First Division Museum.)

Six

Honoring All the Veterans of World War II from Kane County

The enormity of World War II worldwide and nationally is historically documented with both civilian and military personnel losses. Total fatalities range from 60 million to over 80 million if including deaths from war-related disease and famine. Civilians killed totaled up to 55 million. As noted, in World War II, Kane County lost 565 men. Signing up quickly for service following the attack on Pearl Harbor, many made the ultimate sacrifice. Seven men from Kane County died on December 7, 1941, including Seaman 1st Class fireman Eugene Fitzsimmons, who died on the USS *Arizona* along with Robert W. Apple, 1st Class Seaman. Walter Backman is another seaman who lost his life at Pearl Harbor. Many men from Kane County were also in battle in Europe, hitting the beaches at Normandy on D-day, including Pvt. LaVerne Lowry, Pfc. Bruce Juneau, Pfc. Carl K. Musich, and Pfc. Louis Tator. Pfc. Fred Anderson, First Army lost his life fighting through to the end at the Battle of the Bulge with the First Army on December 22, 1944—so close to the end of hostilities. Many men from Kane County died as part of the 129th Infantry, Illinois National Guard in Luzon and Manila in the Philippines, including Pfc. Gene Cook, Company D; Lt. John Kaser; Pfc. Paul Grube; and Pfc. Joseph Gabriel, to name just a few. Sadly, four seamen—Robert Billings, Roy Hopper, George Massier, and Carelton Reynolds—went down with the USS *Indianapolis* when it was sunk by the Japanese on July 30, 1945.

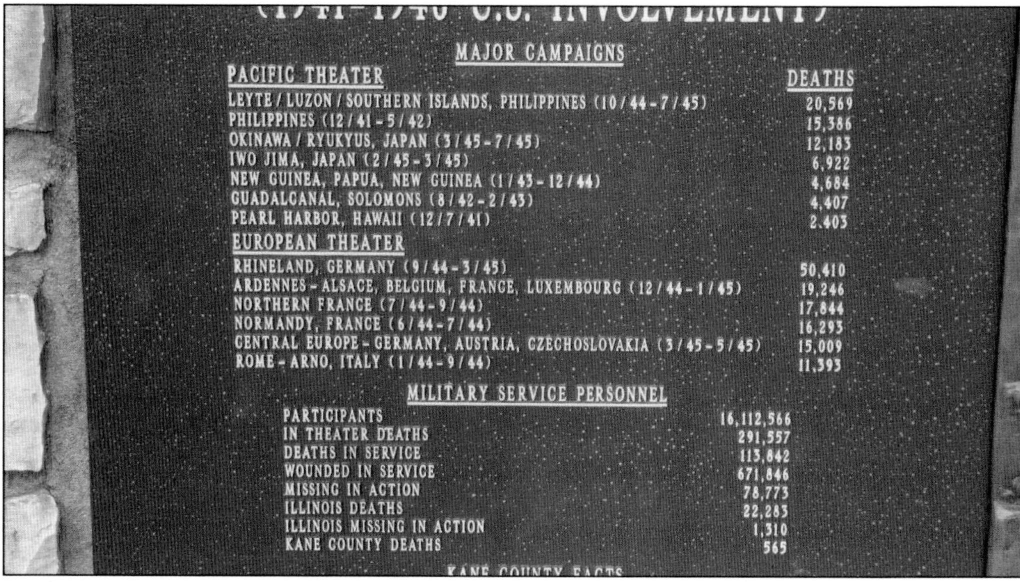

A plaque at the Kane County Veteran's Memorial summarizes the military service personnel lost in major campaigns in both the Pacific and European theaters as well as Illinois and Kane County losses. (Author's collection.)

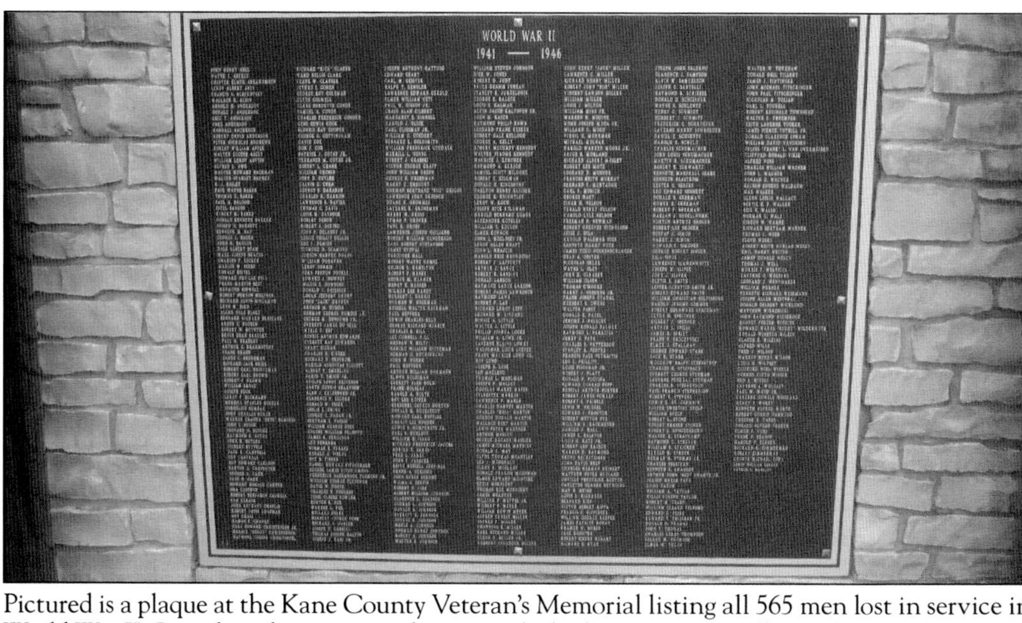

Pictured is a plaque at the Kane County Veteran's Memorial listing all 565 men lost in service in World War II. Specific information and personnel who have served in all wars from Kane County can be found at the Kane County Veterans Memorial website. (Author's collection.)

This was the VFW building constructed quickly following World War II in St. Charles. It represented a coming together of the community and soldiers of both World War I and World War II. The VFW hall was a place of meeting for several years, and the men and women of both VFW Post 5036 and American Legion Post 432 of St. Charles served their community and Kane County as they did in both wars—steadfastly and honorably. (Courtesy of the VFW Post 5036.)

This page from the *Record of Aurora, Illinois in World War II* details service personnel mainly from Aurora, Illinois, who paid the ultimate sacrifice in World War II. The list shows the rank, service, and in most cases, where and under what circumstances the serviceman died. The list captures some of the stories of men such as Seamen Robert Apple and Eugene Fitzsimmons, who both went down on the *Arizona* on December 7, 1941. (Courtesy of J.W. Greenway.)

They Paid the Supreme Sacrifice

Abel, John T/M 1/C "Growler"
Anderson, Fred Pfc. 1st Army Bulge 12/22/44
Anderson, Donald J. S 1/C Atl. Coast Guard 10/22/42
Andrews, Peter Pfc. Co D 2nd Marines—Saipan
Apple, Robert W. F 1/C "Arizona" Pearl Harbor 12/7/41
Ascey, Walter, U.S. Army
Austin, Wm. LeRoy S 2/C "Dorado" Sub.
Backman, Walter S 1/C Lost at Pearl Harbor 12/7/41
Bahrey, Walter S. S 1/C "Extractor" 1/24/45 Pac.
Bailey, N. J.
Balough, Paul A. Lt. 15th Air Force—Anzio Beach
Barnett, Joseph O. T/5/Cpl. 5th Army Anzio Beach
Bangus, Estel Pvt. M P 7th Army
Beam, Dale Albert Cpl. Avn. Killed in Texas 6/8/44
Beatus, Mark Joseph S 1/C "Dan Beard" Pac.
Beitel, Donald TM 2/C Pac.
Best, Frank M. Coc. L.C.S.37 Pac.
Bidwell, Raymond Lt.
Billings, Robert Ens. "Indianapolis" Pac. 7/30/45
Blackman, Paul
Blake, Allan Dale Lt. 12th Air Force
Blassage, Bernard W.O. 2nd Marines Cherry Point, N.C.
Boynton, Robert W. Sgt. 15th Air Force
Brengman, James C. Pfc. Co C. 379th Inf. 9th Army
Brown, Robert Earl Pfc. Timber Wolf Inf. 1st Army—
Buck, Joseph S 1/C Navy
Bruce, Wm. Pfc. Aurora College
Buerer, Merrill Pvt. Co E. 276th Inf. 7th Army
Bumbar, Cornelius Pvt.
Burch, John C. Sgt. 8th Air Force 11/2/44
Busch, John S. Lt. Killed in Hawaii
Butler, John H. Pfc. 11th Arm'd Div. 1st Army 1/14/45
Buttels, Gilbert Died on return home
Carr, George Pvt. Tank Div. Leyte Island
Carr, Jack Lt. 8th Air Force
Carter, Howard Sgt. 609th Q M. 3/18/45 France
Caswell, Robert B. Pvt. 8th Air Force
Chase, Guy S 1/C "Laffey" Pac.
Christoffel, Raymond J. Cox. L.S.T. 531
Clauser, Frank W. S/Sgt. 8th Air Force
Cook, Gene E. Pfc. Co D 129th Inf. Luzon
Cooper, Blonnie R. S/Sgt.
Cox, David
Cox, Don F.
Coyne, Terrance M. Pfc. 48th Arm'd Dic 1st Army
Daraban, George S 1/C "Vincennes" Savo Tel 8/9/42
Daybook, Louis T/Sgt. 8th Air Force
DeBow, Robert Lt. 15th Air Force Africa
DeKing, Robert J. Sgt. Co C. 142nd Inf. 7th Army
Diamond, Sigmond D. CWO Army in Germany
Doane, Judson Harley Lt(jg) "Wasp" Dive Pilot—Pac.
Donavan, Wm. Pfc.
Dorris, LeRoy Pvt.
Downey, Edward J. F O. Army Air Force
Dreissen, Donald J. Lt.
Drury, Logan Jeffery MM L/C "Vincennes" Savo Tel
Dubois, Arthur M. Pfc. Killed in London Air Raid
Dumdic, Herman G. Jr. S 1/C L.S.M. 430 Japan 9/20/45
DuSell, Everett J. Lt. 15th Air Force—Italy
Eby, Robert Cpl. 772nd M P. in camp 8/2/47
Eby, Merle C. Capt. 8th Air Force 6/26/43
Edwards, Everett R. Lt.
Emigh, James T. Sgt. Co A. 751st Tank. Cps. 5th Army
Emmerling, Albert F. Pfc.
Erlanson, G. D. G M 1/C Killed in Aurora
Erlenborn, Alan J. Sgt. 3rd Sig. Co 3rd Marines—Pac.
Esser, Gerald Lt. 8th Air Force 9/10/44—France
Fagan, George Jr. Pfc. Co H. 329th Inf. 1st Army
Fassig, Bertram L. T/Sgt. 8th Air Force
Feldott, Eugene W. Lt. 8th Air Force
Ferguson, James A. Sgt. Army Air Force—Greenland
Ferrara, Leo Lt. 8th Air Force—Germany 11/15/45
Fitzgerald, Daniel H. Pvt. Co D 110th Inf. 1st Army
Fitzsimmons, Eugene J. S 1/C "Arizona" Pearl Harbor
Flannigan, Gerald F Lt. 357th Inf. Hq Co 3rd Army
Fleming, Frederick A. Lt.
Fletcher, Wm. C. MM 2/C "Kimberly"
Foote, David W. Cpl. Co D. 129th Inf. Bougainville
Fowler, J. Claire Lt. 6th Marines "Okinawa" 5/20/45
Fox, Burton K. Lt. Died at Vaughn Hospital 2/14/45
Fox, Warren L. Capt. 8th Air Force France 8/9/44
Gabriel, Joseph Pfc. Hq Co 129th Inf. Luzon 5/4/45
Galvin, Thomas J. Lt. (jg) Navy Air Force 132 Italy
Gari, Joseph J.
Gattuso, Joseph
Geary, Edward
Gengler, Ralph T/5/Cpl. 87th Cav. Merz 1st Army
Geti, Elmer Wm.
Gibson, Paul W. Jr. Lt. Co C. 102nd Inf. 9th Army
Goldsmith, Bernard Pfc. Drowned in Pacific
Goodale, Wm. F. Pvt. Killed in jeep accident in France
Green, John W. S/Sgt. 112th Inf. 1st Army
Gregory, Harry C. Sgt. Tank Div. in Pac. 1/27/45
Grube, Paul R. Pfc. Co D. 129th Inf. Luzon
Gyovai, James Sgt. 8th Air Force—Ireland 4/10/44
Griggs, Norman Ens. Navy Air Force
Groesch, Lawrence J. Pvt. Bty A. 754th F A. 5th Army
Grommes, Duane, H. T/5/Cpl. Hq TGTAS Ft. Knox
Greenman, George E.
Hall, Theodore Lt. Killed in Texas
Hanke, Robert F. Sgt. Co D 123rd Inf. Pac.
Hardy, Wilmer L. Pvt.
Heffner, Paul
Held, Edwin
Hill, Charles S 2/C Died in Bremerton Naval Hosp.
Hill, Leo C. Pfc. Killed in Germany
Hipsack, Richard L. Lt. Alaska Air Force 5/13/48
Hocksprung, Herman C. Pvt. Army 2/3/43 in North Sea
Hoerr, John W. Sgt. Army Air Force in U.S.
Holdiman, Elwyn Cpl. 7th Arm'd Div. 9th Army
Holslag, Frank U S Sp Agent Air Forces in India
Hopper, Roy L. A M 1/C "Indianapolis" 7/30/45
Horton, Hershel G. Lt. 126th Inf. 32nd Div Pac.
Hurlbut, Earl Lt. 15th Air Force Italy
Isaac, William B.
Jackson, Arnold S. S/Sgt. 8th Air Force—Belgium
James, Adrain T.
James, Fred L.
Janecke, John F.
Jericho, Frank A. Pvt.
Jarvis, Wilma J. Lt. ANC Auto accident in California
Jobe, Robert Lt.
Johnson, Donald E. Pfc.
Johnson, Norman H. S/Sgt. 8th Air Force Germ. 6/30/44
Jones, Richard W. T/Sgt. 8th Air Force
Judt, Robert D. Ens. Naval Air Force Killed in Florida
Juneau, Bruce D. Pfc. Killed at Normandy 6/13/44
Jurgelonis, Stanley Pvt. Co C. 180th Inf. 5th Army
Kalman, Louis GM 2/C Killed at Iwo Jima 2/18/45
Kaltofen, Alvin Pfc. Co D. 85th Mt Inf. 5th Army
Kaser, John M. Lt. "Princeton" in the Philippines
Kelly, George A. S/Sgt. 14th Air Force China 5/8/43
Kersch, Raymond S/Sgt. 8th Air Force 12/27/44
Knightley, George R.
Koteles, Alexander Pfc.
Koulous, Wm. S. T/Sgt. 7th Arm'd Div. 1st Army
Kraft, LeRoy Allen Pfc. 1st Rangers
Komes, Harold SC 2/C "Escolar" Sub-Pac.
Kozloski, John L. Jr. T/Sgt. 15th Air Force Vienna
Lafferty, Robert L. Lt. 185th Inf. Pac.
Laws, Raymond
Lawrence, Robert 2nd Marines at Tarawa
Lay, Robert F. Pvt. 1st Sp. Serv. Corps
Little, Walter J. Lt. Cav. & Arm'd Div. 7th Army
Locke, Phillip P. F 1/S "Holder" African Area
Lowe, Wm. A. Jr. Pfc. 1st Marines Pac.
Lowry, LaVerne M. Pvt. 175th Hosp. Normandy
Lund, Frank M. Lt. 1st Marines Avn. 5/11/45

They Paid The Supreme Sacrifice

Malley, Joseph Pfc. Inf. 5th Army
Markus, Sylvester Lt. 10th Air Force in India
Marsh, Lawrence P. T/Sgt.
Martin, Wallace K. SM 3/C "Robalo" Pac.
Martner, Louis P. Plt. Off. 15th Air Force Italy
Massier, George A. S 1/C "Indianapolis" 7/30/45
Mathieu, James M. S 1/C
May, Donald T/Sgt. 8th Air Force
McKnight, Eddie
Mettel, Wm. P. Jr. Lt. Army Air Force So. Carolina
Meyer, Wilbert Pfc.
Meyer, Wm. E. Pvt.
Miller, Channing B. Sgt. 2nd Marines Pac.
Miller, Glenn Pfc.
Miller, Herbert S 1/C 81st N C B. Hq. Opr.
Miller, John H.
Miller, Robert J. Lt. Bombr. 88th Air Force US 8/10/43
Mits, Wm.
Moga, Rome S L/C "Houston" Java Sea 2/28/42
Molnar, Michael S/Sgt. 15th Air Force Austria 2/8/45
Moore, Harold Warren Jr.
Mosley, Richard A. Pfc. 8th Serv Com. Med. Texas
Murtaugh, Bernard S/Sgt.
Musich, Carl K. Pfc. 75th Inf. 1st Army Normandy
Mulligan, James J. S/Sgt. 5th Army Re-enlisted
McAnelly, Clyde Thos. Pfc. M P. Co A Korea
McElroy, Glenn Sgt. Co C. 222nd Inf. 5th Army 1/15/45
McGowan, Donald F. Pfc. 180th Inf. 5th Army
McIntire, E. E. Lt. Co C. 14th Inf.
McKnight, Thomas R. CCM "Belknap" Pac 1/12/45
MacLeod, Ian Lt.
Nagy, George Pvt.
Newman, Freeman N.
Nicholson, Robert G.
Nila, Jesse J. Pvt. Amph. Engrs. New Guinea 5/25/44
Ochsenschlager, James Todd Cpl. Co A 119th Inf.
Oester, Dean A. Pfc. Co 1 318th Inf. 3rd Army
Okler, Nicholas T/5/Cpl. Co M. 123 Rd Inf. Luzon
Oley, Wayne I. Lt. 15th Air Force
Pabst, Walter
Pagel, Donald E. Lt. Died in Jap Prison
Palmer, Joseph R. SF1/C "Neosha"
Paradies, Ray L. T/5/Cpl. 5th Army Italy
Parkhurst, Stewart A. Sgt. 1st Army in the Bulge
Petraites, Francis P. Pfc. Co F 1st Marines Pac.
Phillip, Leo J. Pvt. Bty A 168th AAA.
Piscoran, Louis Jr. France 6/13/44
Platt, Robert J. Lt. 8th Air Force
Pozzi, Raymond Pfc. Banc. 521 U S Marines
Preiss, Arthur T/5/Cpl.
Priegal, Lewis W. S/Sgt.
Proctor, Edward J. Cpl. Co I 335th Inf. 9th Army Germ.
Rackmyer, Wm. A. Sgt. Co D. 29th Div. 1st Army
Rall, Harold
Ratz, Louis R. Pfc. Co L. 253rd Inf. 7th Army 2/8/45
Rausch, Robert Leo S/Sgt. 15th Air Force
Raymond, Warren D. T/Sgt. 9th Air Force
Reep, John David
Reuland, Mathew P. Pfc. Co B. 142nd Inf. Germany
Reynolds, Carleton CPO "Indianapolis" 7/30/44 Pac.
Rhine, Max Capt. Co D. 376th Inf. 5th Army Italy
Richards, Louis Pvt. Bty A 940th F A. 7th Army
Ries, Bernard, Iwo Jima 3/7/45
Rippa, Victor A. MM 1/C "Warrington"
Rippinger, Francis E. Lt. Co C. 60th Arm'd Inf.
Rossiter, Jack Pvt. Died in Calif. Hosp. of Wounds
Rubart, Robert Pfc. Co B 325th Glider Sqd.
Ryan, Richard Cpl. Co C. 782nd Tank Cps. France
Salerno, Joseph John F M 3/C Navy
Sampson, Clarence J. Pfc. 1st Inf. 7th Army
Santelli, Joseph Pfc.
Schlentz, Wayne Lt. 13 & 14th Air Forces
Schmitz, Norbert S/Sgt. 8th Air Force. Died in Germany
Sebers, Lester G. Pvt. Co I 3rd Marines Iwo Jima
Sherman, Donald S. S/Sgt. 8th Air Forces Kriege Prison
Sherman, Homer R. S/Sgt. 8th Air Force over England
Sherman, Robert F. T/4/Sgt. 10th Air Force
Shoellhorn, Harlan J. Lt. 8th Air Force Germany
Shoger, Norton Arthur Pfc. Co A. 397th Inf. 1st Army
Shoger, Robert Lee Pfc. 8th Inf. 1st Army 3/2/45
Singer, George R. Lt. 8th Air Force France
Sipos, Emil
Slawenwhite, Lawrence
Smith, Cletis E. Cpl. 60th Inf. 10/15/44
Smith, Robert E. Pfc.
Solfisburg, Wm. C. Lt. Army Air Force in U S.
Spackman, Robert D. Pfc. 6th Marines Pac.
Spencer, Gilbert Capt. 12th Cav. Luzon
Stallman, Elmer J. S/Sgt. 8th Air Force
Stark, George E. Pvt. Co A. 6th Tank 3rd Army 4/14/45
Starr, Jack R. Cpl. 1st Para Regt. Marines
Stephenson, Chas. B. Sgt. Co C. 407th Inf.
Stephenson, Paul F. Pfc. Co H. 112th Inf.
Stevens, Robert E. Pfc.
St. Germain, Edwin D. Pfc. Marine Aviation Rabaul
Stolp, Foster, S Lt. 8th Air Force
Stolp, Wm. West High
Stone, Robert L. Lt.
Stoner, Robert F. Lt. V C-11 Navy
Stoutenburg, Robert Cpl. B-17 KAAFFGS Louisiana
Strever, Raymond G. Flt Off. 498th Bomb Sqd.
Stricker, Wm. Cpl. Co A. 181st Engrs 1st Army
Strong, Paul Capt. Died in Argentina
Sullivan, Charles Pvt.
Swartz, Arthur John S/Sgt.
Tate, Jeroid M. 1st Sgt. 1st Marines 9/24/44 Pac.
Tator, Louis Pfc. 3rd Arm'd Div. 3rd Army Normandy
Taylor, Willis Eugene Lt. Italy
Taylor, Wm. A.
Teabo, Robert M. Pfc. 5th Army Italy 10/11/44
Telford, Wm. G. S 2/C Navy Air Force
Tesch, Harry G. M/Sgt.
Teske, Edward C.
Thompson, Leland Cpl. Co D. 129th Inf. Philippines
Thomas, Donald O. Capt. 8th Air Corps
Tintinger, James Pvt. Co E. 23rd Inf.
Titschinger, John Paul Sgt. 3rd Tank Div 1st Army
Titschinger, John Michael Pfc. Co D. 3204 Q M
Touvell, Carl L. Ppl. Co F. 127th Inf. New Guinea
Tolian, Nicholas M. S/Sgt. 8th Air Force
Tomlin, Dale E. Lt. 9th Air Force Died in German Pris.
Truemper, Walter E. Lt. 8th Air Force England 2/20/44
Walker, Max.
Walsh, Neil E. Lt (jg) P C 542 Mediterranean Area
Webb, Theo J.
Weeks, Floyd Pvt. 535 C A 1st Army Germany 3/14/45
Weeks, Robert Ens. Ftr Sqd. 80th Air Force
Weiten, Emil H. Sgt. 5th Marines Iwo Jima 3/15/45
Welch, James D. E M 1/C "Albacore"
Wennmacher, Leonard J. S/Sgt. 8th Div. 3rd Army
Westphal, Joseph A. Lost in Pacific
Wildermuth, Howard AMM 3/C
Well, Thomas J.
Werner, Wm.
Wiggins, Rodney Plt. Died in Plane Crash 5/24/44
Wilson, Fred J. CMM "Rabalo" Pacific 9/44
Wilson, Warren Henry
Wiltsey, Lewis Lt. Co B. 53rd Inf. Alaska & France
Winkle, Clifford M. S/Sgt. 15th Air Force Italy 5/24/44
Wolgast, LaVerne S/Sgt.
Woodard, LaVerne H. AOM 3/C Naval Air Force
Worby, Henry J. T/Sgt. 8th Air Force 8/13/44 France
Wurtz, Kenneth F 1/C Sub 28 Hawaii 7/4/44
Yeager, Donald Sgt. Co E. 3rd Div. 1st Army 9/13/44
Zenner, H. P. Lt. 8th Air Forces

The list from *Record of Aurora, Illinois in World War II* conveys the enormity of men lost from Kane County and Aurora. As indicated, many were in various services and major engagements from Europe to the Pacific, including Normandy, Luzon, Italy, Iwo Jima, and in France and Germany. Many lost their lives flying missions for the US Army Air Forces. (Courtesy of J.W. Greenway.)

Seven

Remembering Those Who Served

How a country remembers its veterans both dead and alive reflects directly on the priorities of its government and citizenry. With each passing month and year, another generation of World War II service personnel is passing away. Many communities continue to honor those who served and are serving, even beyond Veterans Day and Memorial Day. The hope and dream of many of the veterans who experienced any war is that there will never be a need for another. In Kane County, there are annual parades and reunions as well as organizations such as the American Legion and Veterans of Foreign Wars still very active. The Kane County Veterans Memorial, situated in front of the Kane County Government Center in Geneva, Illinois, dedicated on November 11, 2004, is a wonderful monument to the men and women who paid with their lives in service to their country. The website states:

> The Kane County Veterans Memorial was conceived in 1997 to honor the men and women of this nation and Kane County who served in the United States Armed Forces. To detail and reflect on the sacrifices made by citizens of Kane County and to honor those county veterans who defended freedom with their lives in the 20th century. The Veterans Memorial remembers and reflects on sacrifices made by Kane County soldier citizens but it is a memorial for all citizens of Kane County with educational and historical references as a reminder that we the people remember and cherish the legacy of freedom, justice, democracy and peace which Kane County veterans have defended.

After World War I, a St. Charles Day parade honored and recognized World War I soldiers and Red Cross nurses from Kane County in July 1919. (Courtesy of the St. Charles History Center.)

This reunion of troops from Elburn and Kane County includes soldiers who served in the Illinois National Guard and the 129th Infantry. (Courtesy of Joseph C. Gaffney.)

These soldiers served in the Illinois National Guard and 129th Infantry. The group was photographed together at Midway Airport in Chicago in 1920. Reunions and veterans organizations became quite popular following World War I. (Courtesy of Joseph C. Gaffney.)

These Illinois National Guard troops marched on June 2, 1919, through downtown Aurora. Col. Charles Green, later a mayor of Aurora, is mounted front and center. (Courtesy of the Aurora History Museum.)

World War I veterans of Kane County reunited at the Elgin VFW Hall in the early 1960s. The group from the Illinois National Guard, 129th Infantry was known as "Elgin's own." The group consisted of 133 volunteers who took part in many of the battles in World War I. The date of the most notable battle, the Battle of the Meuse-Argonne on September 26, 1918, became the date of future reunions. In 1944, at their 25th reunion, the veterans agreed to pass a bottle of Old Grand-Dad Whiskey on to the last living member of Company E. In 1993, Otto Voss drank a toast to all who died before him, and he passed away a month later. (Courtesy of Walter Voss, Elgin Historical Society.)

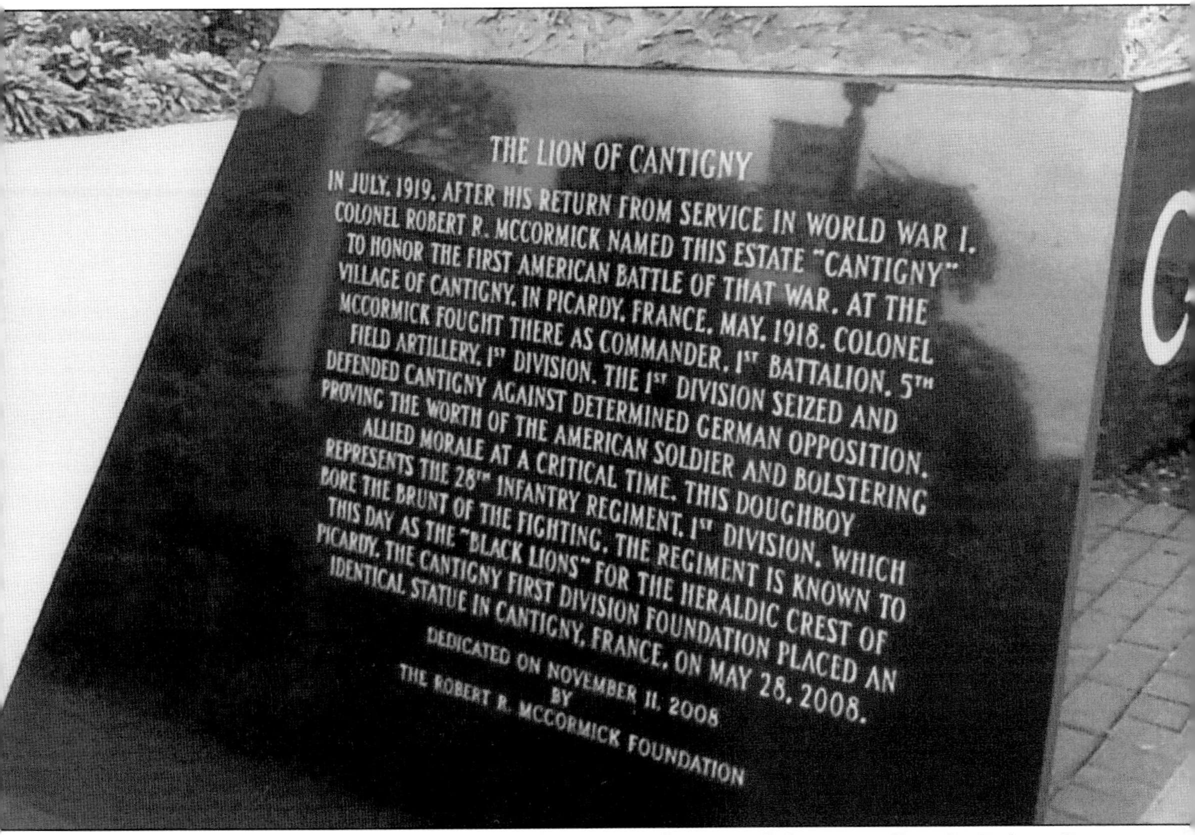

The base of the doughboy statue explains the name *The Lion of Cantigny*. Comdr. Robert R. McCormick named his estate, the location of the museum and exhibits, Cantigny in honor of the men he served with in the 1st Battalion, 5th Field Artillery and all those of the "Big Red," 1st Division. (Courtesy of the McCormick Research Center, First Division Museum.)

The 155-millimeter Schneider howitzer was the US Army's heavy artillery piece during World War I. It could fire a 95-pound shell over six miles. The 1st Battalion, 5th Field Artillery, commanded by Robert R. McCormick, used 155-millimeter howitzers at the Battle of Cantigny, May 28–31, 1918. This cannon, as well as many other tanks and exhibits, is located in front of the 1st Division Museum and Research Center in Wheaton, Illinois. (Author's collection.)

The Spirit of American Youth Rising From the Waves by Donald De Lue is in the south courtyard, behind the 1st Division Museum. The original statue is found in the American Military Cemetery in Normandy, where 9,387 service men and woman are buried. It stands as a tribute to those who gave their lives in the D-day invasion on June 6, 1944. (Courtesy of the McCormick Research Center, First Division Museum.)

Another exhibit on the grounds of Cantigny shows a World War I tank used by the US Army and 1st Division in France and Germany. This tank is an M1917 light tank, which could cross a seven-foot-wide trench and climb a three-foot-high wall. The main gun was a 37-millimeter with a top speed of 5.5 miles per hour. Its weight was 7.25 tons, and it had an armor thickness of .25 inches to .60 inches. Gen. George S. Patton, earlier serving in an M1917 light tank, was a great promoter of the use of tanks in World War I and World War II. (Author's collection.)

Col. Robert R. McCormick speaks at the dedication of the monument at Cantigny, France, in August 1939. His generosity and love of country live on through his estate at Cantigny and the foundation that fosters the history of the 1st Division and all who served so valiantly when called upon. (Courtesy of the McCormick Research Center, First Division Museum.)

The 1st Division Museum and Research Center is also located on the estate of Col. Robert R. McCormick and serves to continually educate the public on the history of the 1st Division. The estate and museum are excellent educational tools for future generations as a reminder of the sacrifices of all personnel during World War I, World War II, and onward. Many of the images contained in this book are from the research center, and many hours and assistance were provided to the author by Mary Manning. Without the generosity of Manning and the museum, this book would not have been possible. (Author's collection.)

BIBLIOGRAPHY

Barry, John W. *The Midwest Goes to War—the 32nd Division in World War I*. Lanham, MD: Scarecrow Press, Inc., 2007.

Gaffney, Kevin J. *While They Were Young-A History of St. Charles and Her Service Personnel, 1940–1945*. New York: iUniverse, Inc., 2009.

General Taylor Collection, First Division Museum, Research Center.

Greenway, J.W. *Record of Aurora, Illinois in World War II*. Aurora, IL: Eugene Smith Co., 1946.

———. *With the Colors from Aurora, 1917–1919*. Aurora, IL: Eugene Smith Co., 1920.

History of the Invasion of France Combat Report, Major Plitt, 16th Infantry, First Division Museum, Research Center. http://www.firstdivisionmuseum.org/research/digital.aspx

Illinois in the World War, Volume I, Chicago States Publication Society, 1920.

Jacobs, Gregory S. *Camp Grant*. Images of America. Charleston, SC: Arcadia Publishing, 2003.

Knickerbocker, H.R. *Danger Forward: The Story of the First Division in World War II*, Nashville: Battery Press, 2002.

Pearson, Ruth Sean. *Reflections of St. Charles, A History from 1833–1976*. Elgin, IL: Brethen Press, 1976.

Smith, Richard Norton. *The Colonel, The Life and Legend of Robert R. McCormick 1880–1955*. Evanston, IL: Northwestern University Press, 1997.

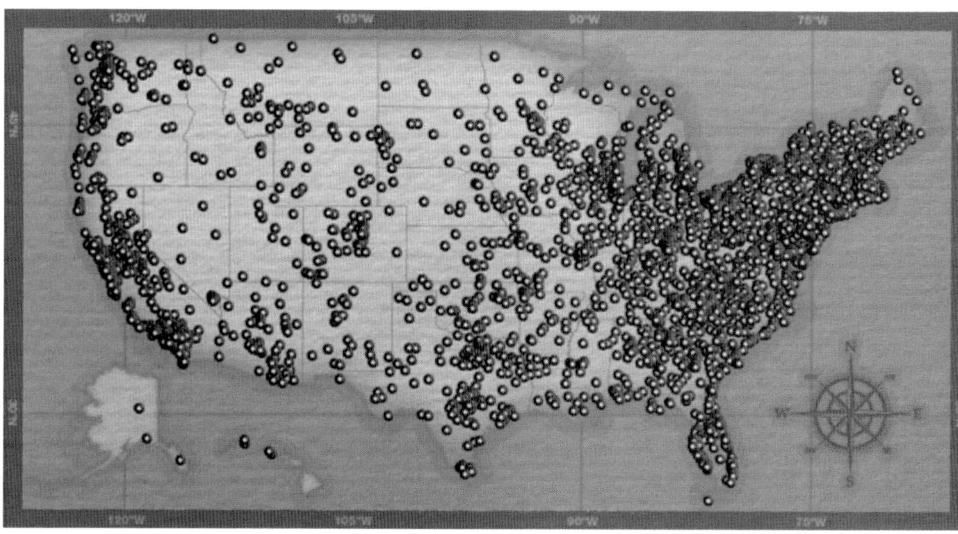